M000072990

Attacking the Elites

Attacking the Elites

What Critics Get Wrong— and Right—About America's Leading Universities

Derek Bok

Yale University Press | New Haven and London

Copyright © 2024 by Derek Bok.
All rights reserved.
This book may not be reproduced, in whole or in part,
including illustrations, in any form (beyond that copying permitted
by Sections 107 and 108 of the U.S. Copyright Law and except by
reviewers for the public press), without written permission from
the publishers.

Yale University Press books may be purchased in quantity for
educational, business, or promotional use. For information,
please e-mail sales.press@yale.edu (U.S. office) or
sales@yaleup.co.uk (U.K. office).

Set in Freight Text Pro type by Newgen North America
Printed in the United States of America.

Library of Congress Control Number: 2023942849
ISBN 978-0-300-27360-1 (hardcover: alk. paper)

A catalogue record for this book is available from the British Library.

This paper meets the requirements of ANSI/NISO Z39.48-1992
(Permanence of Paper).

10 9 8 7 6 5 4 3 2 1

CONTENTS

———

CONTENTS

PREFACE

————

I T WAS MY GOOD FORTUNE IN THE WANING DAYS OF 1970 to receive an invitation to become the twenty-fifth president of Harvard University. For the next twenty years, I did my best to solve the never-ending series of problems that consume a president's day and to make the most of opportunities to improve the quality of the faculty and strengthen our academic programs. Fifteen years after I had retired as president and turned to writing books about higher education, I was unexpectedly asked to serve again for a year after the incumbent president had abruptly resigned. That year gave me what I came to call my "Rip Van Winkle experience," in which I discovered that much in the University had changed, though much was still the same.

During this second term of service, I began to see the effects of the divide between liberals and conservatives, red states and blue states, Republicans and Democrats that would continue to grow in the ensuing years amid the stagnation of middle- and lower-middle-class incomes and the inability of Congress to take vigorous steps to deal with climate change, gun violence, immigration, and other persistent problems in our society.

In this sour environment, there has been little to celebrate in America and much to complain about. Although universities are not directly involved in most of the problems at the center of the nation's controversies, they are not immune from their effects. Elite institutions like Harvard have continued to dominate the lists of the world's greatest universities, but they have hardly been viewed with pride by those who have spoken or written about them for public consumption. The views of critics on both ends of the political spectrum, and even of members of the elites' own faculties and student bodies, have been decidedly negative. The books their scholars write may receive praise, and the discoveries their scientists make may be greeted with awe and admiration, but commentary about the institutions themselves has been consistently hostile.

Equally striking has been the near absence of any response to the criticism by those who speak for the universities under attack. Perhaps their leaders believe that responding to critics would simply provoke more hostile rejoinders. Perhaps they feel that defending these institutions is unnecessary, since they continue to attract huge numbers of applicants for admission and raise hundreds of millions of dollars in gifts every year. Even so, their silence troubles me, not only because many of the criticisms seem mistaken or exaggerated but also because some of them have exposed genuine problems in need of discussion and reform.

Within the past few years, the criticisms have grown louder, and public officials from all levels and branches of government have been more inclined to intervene. We have reached a point at which colleges and universities are at risk of losing their traditional autonomy over the most basic matters of education policy. Since elite universities play a vital role in a world increasingly in need of new knowledge and education of high quality, a careful examination of the complaints against them strikes me as especially useful and timely.

In writing this book, I understand that readers may be skeptical of any treatment of the subject written by someone who has devoted over twenty years of his life to presiding over the oldest and wealthiest of elite universities. I understand their reaction. Nevertheless, ex-presidents have some advantages to bring to such a discussion. They have the benefit of having observed the behavior of these institutions at close hand over an extended period and hence should have a thorough understanding of how they actually work. In addition, once a few years have elapsed since their term in office ended, they no longer feel inhibited from acknowledging flaws in their institution that are in need of correction.

What this book attempts to do, therefore, is to suggest what our leading universities might do to improve by distinguishing the valid complaints against them from the spurious criticisms while also identifying some additional problems that deserve more careful consideration from the elites than they have thus far received.

Attacking the Elites

PART I

———

The Role of Elite Universities
in America

THERE IS NO CLEAR LINE THAT DEFINES AMERICA'S elite universities.* All these institutions, however, share several characteristics: they admit a very small percentage of the students who apply; their faculties include numerous professors who enjoy stellar reputations for their research; they regularly appear in rankings of the twenty-five or thirty most

---

*Let me make clear at the outset that I regret having to use the word *elite* to describe the universities featured in this book, because it has connotations of smugness and superiority that I do not wish to convey. Nevertheless, elite has been used so often to describe the universities in this study that, after experimenting with several substitutes, I had to agree that no other word was equally suited to my purpose. I recognize, however, that there are other colleges and universities that are fully as worthy of praise and recognition for the outstanding work they do. Some in particular have had remarkable success in educating students who are much harder to teach and much more likely to drop out than the academically gifted students who populate our leading research universities. With little money to spend, these institutions literally change the lives of many who come to them for an education. In doing so, they do a different job but one that is just as hard and just as praiseworthy as the work of the more famous universities featured in this book.

highly esteemed universities in America and in the world; and they all have accumulated endowments valued in the billions of dollars. Most of these institutions are private, but a handful of the best state "flagship" universities must surely be included as well. Some would even nominate several of the best independent four-year colleges, since they offer an exceptionally good undergraduate education, attract many more applicants than they can admit, and have substantial endowments. Nevertheless, they are not truly comparable to the leading universities because they neither try to have first-rate research programs nor include professional schools or large graduate (PhD) programs.

The reputation of the leading universities is unusually durable. Almost all of the handful of tiny colleges that were founded before the American Revolution continue to be numbered among the most prominent universities today, while only one current member of the elites has been founded since the end of World War II.

There are obvious benefits to being a leading university. These institutions regularly attract the best students, assemble the most accomplished faculty, and receive the largest philanthropic gifts. They never have to worry about whether they will enroll enough students to keep their doors open or find enough money to survive the next recession.

What is much less often discussed are the obligations that accompany these advantages. Critics simply assume that elites should do whatever the critics would like them to do. This is a weak basis for holding them accountable, especially if the responsibilities involved would cost a lot of money or interfere with achieving the other important responsibilities they perform for educating students and carrying out research.

Accordingly, I consider several questions: Why has America welcomed the development of elite universities, and what obligations do these institutions assume by virtue of their good fortune? How well have elites performed in fulfilling society's expectations, and why can their leaders take great satisfaction from their accomplishments? Answering these questions will provide a foundation for subsequent chapters that evaluate the criticisms of liberals and conservatives concerning the behavior of these exceptionally fortunate universities.

CHAPTER 1

———

Why Have Our Leading Universities Been So Successful, and What Responsibilities Do They Owe in Return?

EARLY IN MY PRESIDENCY, AS I BEGAN TO READ ABOUT the educational systems in other parts of the world, I realized that the presence of a few universities of exceptional quality is not a common feature of most contemporary systems of higher education. Great Britain is home to Oxford and Cambridge, but in most European countries, such as Sweden, Germany, Italy, the Netherlands, and Spain, universities are much more equal in status, resources, ability of students, and research accomplishments. In very few nations are *private* universities as prominent as they are in the United States, and only in America and England do such institutions regularly dominate the lists of the most highly regarded universities in the world.*

*Oxford and Cambridge both receive public funds from the British government, but they are self-governing, the bulk of their resources are private, and their faculties are not civil servants or appointed by the government, as they are in most of Europe.

The wealth of the United States—together with America's exceptionally strong philanthropic tradition—has helped elite universities prosper by soliciting donations large and small. This beneficence is not distributed equally among our institutions of higher learning. Far from it. Twenty institutions, most of them private, together possess almost half of the total endowments owned by colleges and universities; just four account for a full one-quarter. Large differences in wealth and status also exist within state systems of public higher education. In most states, one or two flagship research universities collect the bulk of all gifts to public universities and regularly receive the highest per-student appropriations from their state legislature as well as the largest share of research support from the federal government.

Great wealth goes hand in hand with first-rate research, excellent facilities, and a reputation for excellence. It is no accident, then, that the richest American universities tend to attract the most academically talented students and the most distinguished scientists and scholars. The quality of their students and faculty in turn makes them especially attractive to large donors, major foundations, and government agencies.

The prominence of this small group of colleges and universities gives rise to several questions that are rarely if ever considered explicitly in discussions of higher education. How should we judge a system of higher education in which a few colleges and universities are so successful and accumulate such great wealth and prestige? Is it a good or a bad thing that so many people in positions of power and influence have graduated from this same small group, whether from their colleges, their professional schools, or both? And finally, what special obligations do such wealth and success impose on these favored institutions? What do they need to do to justify their good fortune?

THE ARGUMENT FOR HAVING ELITE UNIVERSITIES

The justification for a system of higher education marked by such great inequality ultimately rests on the proposition that a few individuals, both students and adults, have exceptional ability to produce lasting and important additions to knowledge or to make other significant contributions to society in later life. This proposition is amply supported by experience and has long been accepted as valid, although there are differences of opinion over how to identify such potential in deciding which young people to admit to study in these institutions.

In research, it is intuitively obvious that the nation will benefit if the most accomplished and most promising scientists and scholars have the best facilities in which to do their work. It is also likely that first-rate scientists and scholars will normally be most productive if they can work in proximity to outstanding colleagues with whom to converse, collaborate, and collectively attract the ablest graduate students. Similarly, it seems likely (though not yet proven) that the most accomplished scientists and scholars will be most successful in the classroom when they teach exceptionally talented students. For these reasons, having a limited number of universities with especially talented faculties and students is generally thought to improve the process of discovery and innovation.

The proposition that elite universities can know enough to choose the students most likely to lead influential lives is more problematic. Of course, no one can be certain which seventeen- or eighteen-year-olds possess the greatest potential to make important contributions to society after they graduate. Nevertheless, the assumption is that experienced admissions officers can discover enough information to select young people who not only possess unusual intellectual ability but have also demonstrated exceptional qualities of initiative, self-discipline, determination, and other dispositions that augur well for success in later life. Admittedly, this process does not work perfectly. There are certainly many adults who have had outstanding careers without having attended a leading university and many students who appear to have great promise yet accomplish little in later life. Still, the exceptional number of highly successful and productive adults who have studied at these few prominent universities lends some plausibility to this underlying assumption.

The third proposition is that young people who show the greatest potential for making significant contributions in later life should receive the best available education because the society as a whole will benefit as a result. This assumption seems sound enough in principle, but it suffers from the fact that we know less than most people think about what constitutes the "best" education and whether leading universities are truly providing better preparation than other universities with fewer resources. To be sure, leading colleges have the highest graduation rates, and their alumni tend to earn larger salaries and are more likely than the graduates of other institutions to occupy prominent positions and make important contributions in later life. Yet whether these favorable outcomes are the result of a better education or merely reflect the superior talents that students brought with them when they entered college has not been definitively resolved. The best guess is that both contribute to the final result, but this is only a guess.

Although I have little hard evidence to prove the point, my years at Harvard left me with two additional beliefs about the advantages to society from having a few colleges and universities that consistently attract disproportionate shares of the most academically talented students. One of these impressions is that going to college with classmates of exceptional academic ability, many of whom have already accomplished remarkable things, tends to lift the ambitions of all the students and to increase the likelihood that they will strive harder to succeed in their careers and to accomplish something significant than they might have done if they had been scattered more widely among the 2,800 four-year colleges in the United States.

My second impression is that living and competing with other students of high intelligence and academic accomplishment who also aspire to the most desirable jobs and admission to the top graduate and professional schools cause many undergraduates in these favored colleges to spend more time preparing for their classes and exams than students at most other colleges. This impression was borne out by one survey of Harvard undergraduates that discovered that our students had not experienced the large decline in hours of study per week displayed by most other students nationwide. There is some evidence that this tendency is true for other leading colleges as well.[1]

The ample resources of these favored institutions and the quality of their students and faculties enable them to attract the most promising young scientists and scholars for graduate study, not only from America but from other countries as well. Today, half or more of the PhD candidates in many of America's best science and engineering departments come from other countries, and substantial percentages remain here for at least several years after they graduate. Even students from abroad who return to their own countries often retain links to laboratories and research teams in the United States and collaborate in important ways with projects undertaken here. The ability to attract these able young people from around the world is crucial for America, which has never produced as many exceptionally talented individuals as it needs. Even our best universities did not acquire their dominant reputation in the world until the wave of scientists and scholars fleeing Hitler began to arrive in America during the 1930s.

By attracting talented students from around the world, elite universities also play an important role in the growth of international networks of public officials and corporate executives who share a common experience of graduate study in America. The resulting effects are difficult to measure, but it seems intuitively likely that such ties are advantageous to the United States as it strives to prosper in an increasingly competitive global environment. For example, one would assume that it was helpful when the international cartel of oil-producing nations (OPEC) was first formed that its chief negotiator had studied at Harvard Law School and that in the meetings with Iranian officials that led to the treaty limiting its nuclear program, a leading Iranian negotiator had done his graduate work at MIT.

These thoughts about the value of especially favored universities are necessarily somewhat speculative since this subject has not attracted much careful scholarly attention. It is worth noting, however, that in recent years, China, Germany, and several other countries that have heretofore lacked elite universities have begun to invest more heavily in a small number of institutions in the hope that they will eventually be ranked among the best in the world. In China, Tsinghua University and Peking University appear to have already achieved this goal.[2]

THE OBLIGATIONS OF ELITE UNIVERSITIES

Most of the critics of our leading universities do not discuss why these institutions, most of which are private, should feel obliged to assume special responsibilities beyond what the laws require, even though the reforms these authors recommend would often be very costly. They simply argue that their proposals would achieve a better, fairer result without giving any other reason why elite universities should be expected to go to the trouble and expense of following their advice.

It is not immediately obvious, however, why elite universities—or at least the great majority of them that are private institutions—should have any obligations beyond the duty of all organizations to obey the law and fulfill the promises they have made on which their students and others have relied. After all, there is little talk about the social obligations of private schools, country clubs, or resort hotels. Why should private elite universities be treated differently?

A few authors seem to argue that it is because these universities benefit handsomely from government subsidies, student aid, and exemption from federal, state, and local taxes that they acquire a broad duty to act in the public interest.[3] The problem with this rationale is that governments are already receiving a lot in exchange for the benefits they have conferred on these universities. Research grants are paid for by the discoveries of academic scientists, which contribute to economic growth and benefit the public in other ways. Federal financial aid is more than recompensed by the numbers of students in private universities who would otherwise have to be educated at public expense. The forgone revenue for city governments resulting from property tax exemptions is usually more than compensated by the additional taxes paid by businesses, their employees, and other well-to-do families that locate in the neighborhood in order to be near a major research university. The efforts that several state governments have made to strengthen their flagship institutions in the hope of creating another Silicon Valley testify to the economic benefits that leading universities can generate.

A number of eminent universities may be thought to have tacitly acknowledged the burdens they create for the surrounding city by making "in-lieu-of" payments to partially offset the inability of local governments to collect real estate taxes on university land. This notion is also not convincing. No sensible person would contend, for example, that Cambridge or Boston would prosper more if Harvard and MIT did not exist. Leading universities do not pay in-lieu-of taxes because they owe the city a debt. They do so because they wish to be good neighbors and because the city can make life very uncomfortable for any university that does not cooperate. The pressure that local officials can exert is much enhanced by the fact that universities cannot move, as corporations can, if the city's demands seem unreasonable.

There must be some other basis than tax exemptions, then, on which to establish the duties owed by a leading university to the public. In fact, there are two kinds of responsibilities that our elite universities need to honor. The most obvious obligations are those that are held in common with other persons and organizations, such as the duty to comply with the laws the government imposes, the responsibility not to endanger the health and safety of others, and the obligation to live up to the representations they have made about their programs and services on which students, faculty, and staff often rely in choosing to enroll or accept an appointment.

The second set of obligations includes those that exist because elite universities have had the good fortune to attract exceptionally talented faculties, amass abundant resources, and enroll students of unusually great ability and promise. Because of these advantages, elites assume certain civic responsibilities either from a sense of noblesse oblige or from a desire to gain goodwill or forestall intervention by the government.

One such responsibility, which derives from the exceptional capability of the faculty for conducting research, is for professors to make their findings public and contribute their specialized knowledge, where appropriate, to inform the public debate about important subjects. This responsibility, by and large, seems amply fulfilled and needs no further discussion here, since most professors have a strong desire to publish their ideas quite apart from any obligation to do so.

Other responsibilities assumed by elite universities have to do with education and derive from the ability of these institutions to enroll a disproportionate number of students possessing unusual qualifications to make significant contributions to society in their later lives. Several of these responsibilities involve the way leading universities select their students from the large and growing numbers of applicants who seek to enroll. One such obligation arises from the boost that elite graduates appear to acquire in their careers by having been selected from a large pool of applicants and educated by a highly accomplished faculty. In order to provide this advantage more equitably, a number of elite colleges have begun to make special efforts to identify and recruit able students from low-income families. This is not a legal or an enforceable obligation but a responsibility that these universities have assumed voluntarily because it will further the "American Dream" of allowing young people a more equal opportunity to succeed according to their abilities and ambitions. This goal enjoys wide support not only because it seems fair but also because society as a whole will benefit if young people are not prevented from achieving their full potential by the handicaps resulting from the limited resources of their parents. What is not so clear is how vigorous and expensive an effort elites should undertake to recruit such students and subsidize their education. This issue is explored at length in chapter 3.

Another responsibility that all elite universities have assumed is to diversify the racial composition of their student bodies by making special efforts to recruit, admit, and educate substantial numbers of Black, Latino, and Native American applicants. Many people assume that elite universities have made this effort in order to counteract the existence of racial prejudice or atone for the way society has mistreated these groups in the past. In fact, however, universities have other important motives for making efforts of this kind. One of them is to help all their students learn to live and work harmoniously with people from other races. Another reason is the need to help America avoid the frictions and resentments that might befall a society in which the leadership in government, business, the professions, and the military is largely made up of Whites while the rest of the population grows increasingly diverse.

The benefits derived from educating a more racially diverse student body are not universally appreciated by the larger society. In fact, the policy of affirmative action embraced by elites in admitting minority students has been vigorously contested, with results that are discussed at length in chapter 7.

Finally, like all colleges and universities, elites should offer the best education they can, given their resources and their other responsibilities. In addition, because elite colleges tend to attract undergraduates of exceptional ability and promise, several specific aims assume a special urgency and importance while others become less significant. In view of the fact that the vast majority of undergraduates in leading universities go on to acquire an advanced degree in a professional school or PhD program, their colleges do not need to heed the frequent calls from politicians to emphasize vocational programs that will prepare their students for jobs. What they do need to do, however, is to provide an education for their undergraduates that accomplishes at least three other objectives.

First of all, because their students have exceptional ability and promise, it is particularly important that elite universities give them as much help as possible in choosing the calling to which they will devote their working lives. By this, I mean not merely establishing a conventional placement office but making an additional effort to offer students opportunities to explore alternative vocations, participate in discussions about different careers with fellow students, and learn from adults who have pursued various callings.*

Second, because many of their students are likely to hold positions in later life that have significant effects on the lives and welfare of others, it is especially important that elite colleges try to help all their students develop a strong character and good ethical judgment—an ability to perceive ethical questions when they arise, think clearly and carefully about how to resolve them, and try to act in accordance with their conclusions.

Finally, elites ought to encourage their students to develop a strong sense of civic responsibility. Of course, since almost all those who enter college will be citizens of this country, every university needs to provide such preparation for their undergraduates. Once again, however, this responsibility is especially important for elite universities because so many of their students will eventually play an influential role in the larger community. Hence, the civic education they provide should involve more than an introductory course that teaches students about the various branches of government. Of particular importance is the need to convey an understanding of the strengths and vulnerabilities of our system of government and the role of active and informed citizens in building strong communities, strengthening civil society, and preserving a successful democracy. In addition, elite

---

*I discuss this subject in greater detail in my book *Higher Expectations: Can Colleges Teach Students What They Need to Know in the Twenty-First Century?* (2020), pp. 80–95.

universities ought to offer a wide variety of community service activities that will help their students acquire a commitment to serve others as well as gain practical experience in the kinds of problems that society need to address.

THE BURDEN OF SUCCESS

Elite universities enjoy many benefits from their enviable reputations and avoid many problems because of their considerable wealth. At the same time, they acquire some special burdens. Because they educate a disproportionate share of the leaders and influential members of society, they are likely to be held at least partly responsible for much that is felt to be inadequate, misguided, and unjust in America. During times like the present, when large majorities of the public feel that the country is moving in the wrong direction, leading universities are likely to find themselves the object of criticism from commentators who claim that they are somehow partly at fault.

Elite universities are consequently in a precarious situation at present. If they are to protect their reputations and avoid unwelcome regulation, they need to pay close attention to their critics, acknowledge any flaws or deficiencies in their performance, and pursue whatever opportunities they have to improve what they are doing and demonstrate their value to society. These matters are the subject of the remaining chapters of this book. Before commencing our analysis, however, it will be helpful to begin by taking stock of all the ways elite universities are already helping serve their students and our society. Accordingly, the following chapter explains why most presidents of elite universities will insist that their institutions are currently accomplishing a lot to benefit the nation.

CHAPTER 2

———

A View from the Bridge

Why Elite Presidents Are Proud of Their Universities

PRESIDENTS OF ELITE UNIVERSITIES HAVE GOOD reason to take pride in the performance of their institutions.[1] The list of their accomplishments is undeniably impressive.

By any measure, the quality of research in America's leading universities is outstanding. It has won them a place at or near the top of every list of the world's leading academic institutions in every field of knowledge, whether the rankings are compiled in America or by organizations in other countries. In 2022 eight of the top ten universities in the world and fifteen of the top twenty-five were American, according to the *Times* of London, while half of the top ten and thirteen of the top twenty-five were included on a similar list compiled by a Chinese institute.[2] The same is true of lists of the most innovative universities or the institutions whose faculty have spawned the highest number of new businesses.[3] Americans have won more Nobel Prizes in science and economics than their counterparts in any other nation, and many of the prizewinners from other countries have either studied or taught at an elite American institution.[4] By virtue of these accomplishments, our leading universities have come to play a vital role in the development of new products, new treatments for disease, and the promotion of economic growth.

The reputation of elite universities for educating students is no less impressive. At a time when enrollments in all American colleges have been declining, elites have continued to attract growing numbers of students every year. As a result, they now have many times the number of applicants they can accommodate: Harvard and Stanford now accept fewer than 4 percent of all those seeking admission.

It is not possible to know precisely how well our leading universities have fulfilled their responsibility to educate students with exceptional potential for contributing to the welfare and progress of society. Such evidence as we have, however, suggests that they have been quite successful in admitting and graduating unusually promising young people who go on to live lives of unusual prominence. If one examines the lists of individuals who have won Rhodes Scholarships and Nobel Prizes, been selected for high positions in government, included in *Who's Who*, become the CEO or served on boards of major corporations, started new and successful businesses, become partners in major law firms and judges in the highest courts, been chosen to lead important nonprofit organizations, or even been the authors of prizewinning books, the percentages that have studied at the colleges and professional schools of elite universities are far above the average for graduates of other educational institutions.[5]

There is no reliable way to measure how much students learn during their undergraduate years, but several findings suggest that students in elite colleges gain a great deal from their education.* Once graduated, they tend to earn significantly more on average than the graduates of other colleges. Most of their success probably derives from qualities they brought with them when they entered college. Still, controversy continues over the effects of selectivity and whether graduates of elite colleges tend to earn more than other graduates after taking full account of differences in the academic ability and ambition of students when they entered college.[6]

Elite universities spend far more per student than other colleges on the education of their undergraduates.[7] The results reflect the effects of these expenditures. Graduates of these institutions also tend to be well represented among the colleges with the highest rates of alumni satisfaction. They also finish college and receive diplomas at much higher rates than students from other colleges. While the nation's completion rates from four-year colleges hover around 60 percent—a figure lower than that of several other highly industrialized nations—most elite private institutions graduate over 90 percent of their entering students.

Despite spending far more per student on undergraduates than other colleges, elite faculties have often been accused of neglecting their teaching in order to devote more of their time to research. There are growing signs, however, that any such

---

*According to one widely cited study, students in the most selective colleges tend to devote more hours per week to their classes and coursework and improve their writing and critical thinking skills more than students at other colleges. Richard Arum and Josipa Roksa, *Academically Adrift: Limited Learning on College Campuses* (2011), pp. 72, 93. Similar findings are reported by Wendy Fischman and Howard Gardner on the basis of interviews with several thousand college students; *The Real World of Colleges: What Higher Education Is and What It Can Be* (2022), pp. 129–30.

tendency has diminished or even disappeared in recent years. Recent surveys find that elites dominate the lists of colleges with the most satisfied alumni.[8] There were indications even before the coronavirus pandemic that growing numbers of elite professors were making increasing use of their teaching and learning centers to improve their methods of instruction. By 2017, for example, almost one hundred tenured faculty were using the services of the Harvard center every year. This tendency accelerated greatly when the coronavirus pandemic struck and forced college instructors to adapt immediately to online teaching. Doing so has made instructors more comfortable with using technology and led them to spend more time experimenting with ways that rely less on simply lecturing online to a passive audience and make more use of small group problem-solving and active discussion, often using the new technology.[9] This experience in turn has given rise to major efforts to explore how technology can be employed to vastly expand the audience for universities by reaching new students in America and overseas who are interested in gaining access to an elite university education but cannot come to campus to enroll in a residential program. Where all this will lead is hard to predict, but it surely tends to refute the oft-repeated charge that professors in elite research universities do not really care about undergraduate education.

Elite universities have also recognized that they have responsibilities beyond simply educating the most accomplished and most promising students they can find. They have made substantial efforts to promote economic mobility and greater equality of opportunity by actively recruiting and admitting more students with academic potential who have not had the advantages enjoyed by their traditional undergraduates. Over the past sixty years, they have made strenuous efforts to attract minority students through vigorous recruitment and the use of racial preferences in deciding whom to admit. More recently, they have also begun to enroll more students from low-income families. To achieve this goal, they have expanded their financial aid programs to such a point that in several elite universities, students whose parents earn below the nation's median income need not pay any tuition and can graduate without any debt. Because of these reforms, low-income students can enter and graduate from the most selective colleges in the country for less money than they would have spent to attend their local community college.

Even with this generous financial aid, elite universities have found it harder than they expected to locate talented low-income students and persuade them to apply. Those who have sufficient academic credentials to do well in an elite college are relatively few and widely scattered geographically. Some may not want to leave their families and enroll in an elite college. Others may view elite colleges as remote and forbidding places. Nevertheless, progress has been made, and the numbers of students in several leading colleges who come from families in the lower half of the income scale have gradually risen to reach 20 percent or more of the entire entering class.

The results of diversifying the student bodies of elite colleges have been both substantial and costly. The figures from Harvard's entering class in 2022 are illustrative. In that year, Harvard accepted 1,954 (or only 3.2 percent) from the record-breaking 61,220 students applying for admission. Some 55 percent of those admitted qualified for financial aid and would pay only an estimated average of $12,000 per year for their education, room, and board, although the full yearly cost for students whose parents were wealthy enough to afford it exceeded $76,000. Twenty percent of those admitted would not have to pay anything for college, since the incomes of their families were below $75,000 per year. By working a modest amount in term time or at summer jobs, they could graduate free of any debt whatsoever. The class was also racially diverse: approximately 15 percent identified as Black, 12 percent as Hispanic, and 28 percent were Asian American.[10]

The cost to Harvard was far from trivial. During the fifteen years following its decision to increase the funding for low-income students, the University spent almost $3 billion on financial aid for undergraduates. Over this period, the total cost of need-based financial aid grew from $80 million per year to $230 million in 2022–23. As a result, Harvard, along with most private elite universities, is among the few institutions in America that have made college affordable for all their undergraduates while keeping their debt loads remarkably light.

Whether or not our leading universities are doing enough to fulfill their responsibilities to the nation, readers may wonder if it is a good thing that so many prominent figures in different fields of endeavor have been educated in the same small group of universities. Commentators have recently expressed some concern over the fact that eight of the nine Supreme Court justices attended either Yale or Harvard Law School, while five of the last six presidents were educated at Ivy League universities.

In America, however, there is considerable variety within the ranks of our leading universities. Caltech, U.C. Berkeley, and Yale differ significantly from one another in the undergraduate experiences they provide. Certainly, the alumni of elite universities are by no means all alike in their thinking. Justices Samuel Alito and Sonia Sotomayor may both have graduated from Princeton and attended Yale Law School, but they hardly have the same judicial philosophy. Liberal members of the Senate, such as Ted Kennedy, Chuck Schumer, and Barack Obama, all attended Harvard, but so did conservative Republican senators, such as Ted Cruz, Tom Cotton, and Josh Hawley.

The value of America's elite universities cannot be truly understood by simply tabulating the accomplishments of their faculty members, students, and alumni. Such figures do not capture the full variety of benefits these institutions provide to America and the world.

Elites are often caricatured as ivory towers, insulated from the actual problems of society. It is true that there are plenty of professors and classes that deal with abstract problems or devote themselves to the study of ancient languages and civilizations, obscure theoretical questions, learned critiques of arts and culture, and new interpretations of centuries-old historical periods. These are all worthy fields of study, however irrelevant they may seem to those who value universities solely for their ability to prepare students for jobs and produce innovation to spur economic growth. Yet even viewed from a strictly practical perspective, elite universities are immensely important for the tangible benefits they provide.

There is scarcely a critical problem in America or the world that has escaped the attention of the faculties of elite universities. Whether the subject is the threat of global warming, the effects of social media and artificial intelligence, the influence of nutrition on health and longevity, mass migration, the scourge of poverty and homelessness, the development of new and improved technologies, the causes of and cures for disease, the reasons for inflation and recession, or even the nature and sources of happiness, there are professors engaged in analyzing the problem and suggesting appropriate improvements.

Meanwhile, far from being sheltered from the "real world," massive numbers of students are participating in projects and programs involving all sorts of problems facing society. In most elite universities many hundreds of undergraduates are currently volunteering to serve in homeless shelters, work in food banks, tutor children in public housing projects, or assist the teachers in local schools. In professional schools, law students offer free legal services to clients of limited means, assist immigrants seeking to avoid deportation, help settle marital disputes, represent tenants facing eviction, or work in other ways to meet the legal needs of individuals too poor to afford a lawyer. Medical students assist professors in studying a host of diseases or participate in caring for patients in teaching hospitals. Architecture students work on projects to find new and better ways to design energy-efficient office buildings or low-income housing in America or overseas. The list of such activities goes on and on.

All in all, therefore, America's leading universities have much to be proud of. By their accomplishments in research, the quality of their students, the success of their graduates, and their efforts to expand opportunities for talented students from oft-neglected segments of American society, they have achieved most of what the nation can legitimately expect of its leading universities. With the help of their large endowments, they have been able to avoid the two greatest problems affecting American higher education today: the lagging percentages of American youth who graduate from college and the constantly rising cost of attendance that has made going to college seem unaffordable for many young people and their families. Problems remain that elites have not yet solved, and flaws in their behavior exist that need to be addressed. These subjects will be discussed in the next several chapters. These deficiencies, however, must be viewed against the backdrop of a wide array of outstanding accomplishments.

PART II

———

The Liberal Critique

OT EVERYONE ASSOCIATED WITH OUR LEADING
universities is as positive about these institutions as
their presidents. Some of the most prominent critics
are liberals from elite faculties and student bodies. Interestingly,
however, none of their most serious complaints has to do with
improving the quality of teaching or the lives of students. Rather,
the principal aim of liberal critics has been to persuade their universities to become a more active force for promoting justice,
equality, and the welfare of people in America and throughout
the world.

The most widely publicized criticism from liberal professors
has been directed at the way elite institutions decide which students to admit for study. The charge these critics make is that
despite the extremely generous financial aid these universities
provide to needy students, the admissions process works in many
subtle ways to favor the children of wealthy parents over applicants from low-income families. As a result, far from expanding the opportunities for upward mobility and helping fulfill the
promise of the American Dream, leading universities are accused
of perpetuating a hereditary aristocracy of wealth. Professors who

make this claim have suggested several ways to solve the problem but have rarely paused to examine their proposals carefully, even though they would cost a great deal and have far-reaching effects on the universities involved.

Chapter 4 has to do with movements that are typically initiated by ad hoc groups of students from leading universities although they often attract support from sympathetic faculty and alumni as well. These student-led campaigns seek to persuade presidents and trustees to have their institutions play an active role in combating suffering and injustice in the world by divesting their endowments of stock in companies that do business in repressive countries or engage in harmful activities such as degrading the environment or selling dangerous, habit-forming drugs. After reviewing the pros and cons of divestment, the discussion concludes by suggesting better procedures for evaluating student demands in order to reflect the considered judgment of all the constituencies of the university.

The third and last chapter in this section considers the proposals made by Black students and faculty from several elite universities that their institutions acknowledge their past ties to slavery and to other forms of discrimination against Black people and offer some sort of reparations to atone for their complicity. The chapter pays particular attention to the nature and extent of a university's moral responsibility for previous actions and activities linking the institution to evils and injustices in the outside world.

CHAPTER 3

Choosing Whom to Admit to Elite Universities in an Age of Extreme Inequality

L IBERAL CRITICS, MOST OF THEM PROFESSORS AT ELITE universities, have published a number of books and articles that find fault with the admissions practices of these institutions.[1] Although each of these critics defines the harm these policies do in somewhat different ways, all of them agree that a common flaw in existing practices is that they favor the children of wealthy parents at the expense of applicants whose families have much lower incomes.

At first glance, it may seem odd to criticize elite universities for this problem, since almost all of these institutions offer enough financial aid to their neediest students to enable them to complete their studies without paying anything or incurring any debt. Critics are not satisfied by these financial aid programs, however. They often begin by pointing to careful studies carried out by the Harvard economist Raj Chetty and his collaborators.[2] Chetty discovered that students from extremely low-income families who graduated from highly selective colleges were especially likely to earn very high incomes in later life. Nevertheless, these institutions continued to admit very few low-income students despite their generous financial aid programs. Only 3.8 percent of all those enrolling in Ivy League colleges in 2013 came from families in the bottom quintile of the income distribution. Some elites, such as Princeton and Yale, actually enrolled more students from families in the top 1 percent of the income scale than all their classmates with parents in the bottom 50 percent. As a result, while highly selective colleges did better than most other colleges at helping students from very low-income families become rich in later life, they enrolled so few of these young people that several less prestigious colleges did considerably more to encourage upward mobility because they admitted much larger numbers of low-income students.

Neither Chetty nor other vocal critics devote much thought to explaining why leading universities should feel an obligation to admit more low-income students and what this obligation should entail. Of course, one can make a compelling case for the proposition that highly selective colleges should make *some* serious effort to increase their admission of low-income students to further the American Dream of giving an opportunity for all people to achieve success according to their ability and ambition. But how many low-income students these colleges should admit and how they should combine this effort with their obligation to select the students most likely to make a significant contribution to society are not immediately obvious.*

---

*Some critics seem to imply that ultra-selective colleges should admit a proportion of low-income students equal to the proportion of low-income young people among all recent high school graduates. Such a goal is clearly inappropriate, however, because academic ability is not evenly distributed throughout the high school population. A more plausible goal would be to admit the same proportion as the percentage of recent high school graduates who have the academic ability to succeed in a highly selective college and the desire to enroll in such a college. The percentage of high school graduates who meet these two requirements is a matter of dispute. See p. 39.

Critics pay little attention to these questions or to other practical issues, such as how many talented low-income students would want to apply to a highly selective university and how many of them would flourish there. They simply assume that many more low-income students should be admitted and proceed immediately to critique the various ways in which the criteria currently used by the most selective colleges to choose their students are unfairly biased to favor children from wealthy households.

Opponents of the admissions process, however, have some valid points to make. One of their most common criticisms involves the widely used SAT and ACT tests. These exams are an unreliable predictor of future success that give an unfair advantage to applicants from wealthy families because the parents of these students can boost the scores of their children artificially by paying for tutoring and preparatory courses for the tests that poor families cannot afford.[3] In addition, affluent parents often spend thousands of dollars on counselors to advise their children on how to prepare the most effective application and write the most persuasive essays to maximize their chances of admission. Well-to-do families can also pay for the travel abroad and the internships and community service opportunities that make their children appear to be very deserving candidates. Not least, high-income applicants usually live in affluent neighborhoods with far better schools that spend much more money per student than schools in low-income neighborhoods. These well-financed schools, whether public or private, usually offer more Advanced Placement courses to impress admissions officers and hire many more counselors who can write glowing recommendations for their students.

These are not the only ways in which the admissions practices of highly selective colleges advantage students from affluent families. Legacy preferences that give a nod to children of alumni favor well-to-do applicants since most alumni parents have above-average incomes. Many of these colleges also bend their normal admissions standards to admit the children of wealthy parents who might contribute money to the colleges their sons and daughters attend. In flagship public universities and in some highly selective private colleges as well, presidents and trustees are said to put pressure on admissions officers to admit the children of politicians and other influential people, virtually all of whom are well-to-do.* Even the preferential treatment given to talented athletes by most selective colleges favors the children of prosperous families, since many college sports, such as rowing, lacrosse, rugby, golf, squash, and tennis, do not exist in most of the high schools attended by lower-income students. Together, therefore, current admissions practices do a lot to help rich parents pass their success to their children by giving them advantages for getting into selective colleges that are not available to applicants from low-income families.

CRITIQUING THE CRITICISMS

Most admissions officers would agree in principle, as indeed they should, that selective colleges ought to decide whom to admit on the basis of the talents and accomplishments of the applicants rather than the wealth or the connections of their parents. Measured by this principle, several common practices for admitting students are very hard to defend.

---

*There is little evidence of how widespread this practice is. I should add that during my presidency, I never once contacted an admissions committee about an applicant to Harvard. I had been informed early on that efforts by a president to influence an admissions official would be keenly resented. Of course, I have no knowledge of whether anyone else at Harvard ever contacted the admissions office, but I do know of children of extremely influential parents and alumni who were rejected.

One of the most widely criticized admissions practices is the preference given to children of alumni. No wonder. Such a preference has nothing to do with the quality of the applicant. It can even benefit the children of alumni who have done nothing to help the university since they graduated. By now, however, the advantage awarded by many selective colleges is very slight, often amounting to little more than a tie-breaking factor when two or more candidates have equally promising credentials for admission. In a private study I had done in 2006 when I returned as president, I found that the average board scores of legacy admits at Harvard were slightly *higher* than those of the rest of the class in at least half of the preceding ten years. Yet the fact remains that when admissions officers choose which students to admit from a mass of equally promising applicants competing for the last one hundred places in the entering class, even a slight preference will often make a decisive difference in the chances of many applicants. As a result, any preferences given to children of alumni are arguably unfair.

Many admissions officials may privately agree that legacy preferences are unjustified but fear arousing resentment among their alumni if they abandon the practice. Several colleges, however, such as Johns Hopkins, have already stopped awarding such advantages without suffering a loss of alumni contributions or any other adverse consequences. All selective colleges should do the same and abandon a practice that rightly meets with disapproval from most members of the public.

Another suspect practice is the award of admissions preferences to the children of large donors or even wealthy parents who *might* become donors. Of course, policies that encourage substantial gifts will often benefit future students by funding more scholarships or supporting efforts to improve the quality of education. Campus officials may therefore believe that any policy that encourages donations is thereby absolved of criticism on ethical grounds. On closer analysis, however, such reasoning is highly suspect. The same rationale could be used to justify auctioning off the last fifty places in the entering class to the highest bidder (provided the students who benefit are sufficiently qualified to pass their courses and graduate). It is hard to imagine any college presidents in their right mind who would dare to propose such a practice. Yet the reason for both auctions and donor preferences is the same. The only difference is that the auction makes clear to everyone what the college is doing.

Still another dubious practice that is even more widespread is the use of preferences for promising athletes. The advantages given vary in size depending on the sport. Athletes in the so-called minor sports, such as sailing or squash, tend to receive only slight preferences, if any. But in revenue-producing sports, such as football and basketball, coveted athletes in the few highly selective colleges that compete at the highest level may receive an advantage of 300 points or more on their SAT scores and thus enjoy a greater preference than any other category of applicants, including Black and Latino students.[4] The number of applicants receiving athletic preferences is not trivial in colleges of small or medium size. In Ivy League schools, as many as 15 or 20 percent of the entering class can be advantaged in this way. In small, private liberal arts colleges that field teams in many sports, the percentage may be even higher. Of course, some of these athletes may have high school grades and test scores equal to or above those of most other admitted students, but a large majority will not.

Advocates for admitting more low-income students seldom criticize preferences given for high-profile sports, notably football and basketball, even though athletes in these sports often receive the greatest preferences of any group of applicants in the admissions process. Perhaps critics feel that such a proposal would have no chance of being adopted. Perhaps they overlook these teams because they play the sports most likely to include low-income and minority students. Whatever the reason, it is the award of preferences for other sports such as lacrosse, squash, tennis, and the like that most frequently advantage well-to-do students. Today wealthy parents may even hire a personal coach for their children in the hope that they will become proficient enough to be admitted as athletes to a selective college and perhaps even win an athletic scholarship to spare their families much of the cost of a college education.

Individual colleges cannot unilaterally stop giving admissions preferences in any sport without putting themselves at a competitive disadvantage. But an entire conference of selective colleges could surely agree to limit athletic preferences, as the Ivy League has done, or do away with them entirely. Not many elite colleges have done so, however, even for minor sports—either from inertia, fear of controversy, or simply because of a visceral desire to win on the athletic field or even compete for a national championship. They would do well to reconsider this policy. Although the preferences given for minor sports may be small, they still give many recipients a decisive advantage, just like legacy preferences, for reasons having nothing to do with academic ability.

An additional practice that favors well-to-do applicants is the granting of early admission (in December or January rather than April) for students who apply to a particular college before a certain date. In return for early admission, some colleges require the admitted students to agree not to change their minds and attend another institution. This practice works against low-income students because they may have to commit themselves to attend a college before they can discover which other colleges would admit them and compare how much financial aid each institution would provide.[5]

Colleges argue that early admissions protect students from the stress and anxiety of having to wait until April to know which colleges will accept them. But this peace of mind can be achieved by simply granting early admission without requiring students to make a binding commitment to attend. In that way, low-income students would at least have a chance to compare financial aid offers before finally deciding which institution to enter.

The early decision practice would not matter so much if the chances of gaining admission in April were the same as in December. In fact, however, the odds of being admitted to an early decision college are markedly greater for those who apply early. Even some of the early admission programs that do not require applicants to commit themselves have lower admissions standards in December than they do in the spring and thus give an advantage to well-to-do applicants since they are more likely than low-income students to apply early.

Still another questionable practice is to offer an advantage in the admissions process to the children of faculty or staff. If universities wish to reward their professors or administrators, they can subsidize their housing costs or raise their salaries. But it is needlessly unfair to accomplish the purpose by denying admission to more deserving applicants.

The last but most frequently criticized admissions practice is the use of standardized tests such as the SAT or ACT. These test scores are not strongly correlated with later-life success or even with academic success throughout college. All that they do predict with any significant success are first-year grades. However they are used, critics point out that applicants—especially those from families wealthy enough to afford the expense—can improve their test scores by hiring tutors or taking special classes to prepare them to do well. Estimates vary widely as to how much help such assistance provides. According to the calculations of Julie Park from the University of Maryland, the average boost is only about 35 points, although the gains seem to be somewhat larger for Asian students.[6] The College Board, however, has recently issued a statement that students who work conscientiously at one of the courses to prepare them for the SAT can raise their score by over 100 points. The true significance of preparatory courses, therefore, is still a matter of dispute.

Assailed by widespread criticism of the SAT and ACT, a number of colleges have now abandoned their use altogether while hundreds more have made them optional. Some institutions that still use the tests admit as many high-scoring students as they can to improve their place in the college rankings published annually by *U.S. News & World Report*. A few have actually submitted inflated reports of their average test scores in order to raise their ranking. These practices are clearly unfortunate and should be eliminated.*

Experienced admissions officers at most colleges that continue to accept the tests are aware of their weaknesses. Nevertheless, they maintain that judicious use of test scores can improve decision making and even enhance the admissions prospects of low-income and minority applicants by confirming the abilities of applicants who are home-schooled or come from

---

*Many critics of the tests persist in assuming that they are biased against minority students. Yet a large body of evidence has shown that test scores consistently *overpredict* the likely grades of Black and Latino students. For example, the Bowen-Bok study of race-sensitive admissions involving thousands of students attending twenty-nine highly selective colleges found that Black students who entered these colleges with SAT scores and other background characteristics equal to those of their White classmates finished with a class rank approximately 16 percentile points *below* that of those Whites. William G. Bowen and Derek Bok, *The Shape of the River: Long-Term Consequences of Considering Race in College and University Admissions* (1998), p. 77.

little-known high schools whose grade averages would otherwise be hard to evaluate. A unanimous report by a faculty committee at the University of California recently concluded after a yearlong study that the SAT test was actually serving an important purpose by identifying qualified applicants who would have been excluded on the basis of their grades alone. In fact, the committee found that in 2018 the use of board scores led to the admission of several thousand students to the colleges in the University of California system whose applications would have otherwise been denied. Almost half of these students were from low-income families, and one-quarter were underrepresented minorities. If these conclusions are correct, it is hard to fault admissions officers for continuing to look at test scores so long as they restrict their use to cases where there is good reason to believe that doing so will help to evaluate applicants who have attended little-known schools whose grades are hard to judge or applicants who are home-schooled and have no grades at all.

THE CURRENT PREDICAMENT

In recent decades, the number of students applying to leading colleges has grown to such a point that admissions officers can no longer serve both societal needs and the institutional interests of the universities themselves. In the eyes of many admissions officers and university leaders, however, all the competing interests seem important. As a result, the prevailing tendency has been to try to serve them all by gradually reducing the numbers of legacy admissions and other traditional preferences to make room for more minority and low-income applicants. By now, however, the numbers of applicants to elite colleges have grown so large that any use of the traditional preferences threatens to exclude applicants with greater promise for the future.

My personal opinion is that if choices must be made, the public interest should prevail in selecting students simply because it is the right thing to do and will accomplish more for society than fielding better athletic teams, pleasing alumni, or even receiving a few additional gifts from grateful parents.

Quite apart from my personal preference, there is reason to believe that leading universities as well as the general public will eventually prosper more if admissions officers make clear to everyone that they place the highest priority on the public interest and hence will not continue trying to serve both sets of interests simultaneously. Now that leading universities have become so important to a nation dependent on knowledge and innovation and so much in need of highly educated individuals, they are attracting more attention from the public and closer scrutiny from the government and the media than ever before. As a result, they are increasingly vulnerable to lawsuits and government intervention in matters that were once regarded as immune from outside interference.

In this environment, continuing to try simultaneously to serve both the public and their own self-interest becomes quite dangerous. The quiet effort by many leading universities to give a dwindling but still decisive preference to children of alumni and wealthy parents in hopes that these practices will not be noticed has not succeeded. The admissions policies of leading universities have been clearly exposed to public view through lawsuits over racial preferences. As a result, these universities are being accused of secretly benefiting the rich and helping them become a hereditary aristocracy. Leading universities consequently find themselves in the awkward position of being more heavily criticized than ever over their admissions policies at the very time when they are spending tens of millions of dollars every year to admit more minority and low-income applicants and enable them to graduate at virtually no cost in an effort to increase economic opportunity.

By clinging to practices such as legacy preferences, leading universities have made themselves more vulnerable to outside interference and more distrusted by the public than they deserve. Rather than continue down this path and face a growing risk of harmful government intervention, leading universities will end in a better place by making clear that they put the public interest first by shaping their admissions policies to serve the needs and ideals of the nation rather than their own private interests.

A BETTER APPROACH

Even if leading universities were to follow this advice and do away with early-action admission and all preferences for legacies, children of donors or faculty, and athletes in minor sports along with a limited and judicious use of SAT scores, it is doubtful that many of the additional places created in the most selective colleges would be filled by students from low-income families. Although such students can attend most elites without paying anything, few may apply, and many who do may lack the grades and test scores to be admitted.

A straightforward way to enroll more low-income applicants would be to give them a preference in admissions comparable to what virtually all highly selective colleges have long given to minority students. As with minorities, the life experiences of these students will add to the diversity of the student body and thereby enhance the quality of education for everyone. Moreover, students who grow up poor will often have been raised in single-parent families, lived in neighborhoods beset by crime and drug addiction, and attended schools that are greatly inferior in resources to the schools typically found in more affluent communities. Selective colleges should surely give low-income applicants with strong high school records some extra credit for having displayed the resilience and determination to overcome a series of disadvantages unknown to students who have lived their lives in much more favorable environments.

Until 2000, highly selective colleges rarely gave low-income students any discernible preference in the admissions process. By now, however, it is likely that many, if not most, of these colleges do try to take some account of the special disadvantages that these applicants have had to overcome. Yet little is known about how much of a preference is currently being given, and there is no consensus on how much should be awarded. Under these circumstances, selective colleges need to experiment carefully with awarding preferences to discover how much they can do without putting the students involved at too much risk of failing to succeed.

While an effort of this kind seems promising, there is disagreement over how many qualified high school graduates from low-income families would decide to attend very selective colleges if they were given a chance to do so. In a widely publicized study, two economists, Caroline Hoxby from Stanford and Christopher Avery from Harvard, found that up to 35,000 high school students from low-income families graduate each year with grades and test scores sufficient to compete for admission to the most selective colleges, but that only a few enroll or even apply to an elite school.[7] In a subsequent study, Hoxby claimed that many of these students would apply if they simply received literature from selective colleges describing the institution and inviting them to submit an application.[8] Subsequent studies have not confirmed these findings, however, leaving the actual number of willing, academically qualified low-income applicants in considerable doubt.[9]

There is a good deal of anecdotal evidence that many talented low-income students do not *want* to attend a highly selective college. Admissions officers who have made special efforts to recruit such students believe that it is much more difficult to attract them than one might think. Some of these students cannot imagine that they would actually be admitted. Others may feel that they would not feel welcome or be happy at highly competitive institutions filled with classmates from backgrounds so different from their own. Still others do not want to go to college so far from home or cannot do so because they are needed to stay and help their families.

For reluctant students such as these, merely sending them literature is unlikely to suffice. Admissions officers must track them down and try to convince them to apply. Conducting such conversations, however, is complicated by the fact that the students involved do not appear to be concentrated in a few big cities but are widely scattered. Elite colleges that have sent admissions officials into the field to recruit low-income applicants have thus far either been unable to locate as many of these students as Hoxby's estimate might suggest or have failed to interest a great many of them in applying to a highly competitive college.

One enterprising nonprofit organization, the Posse Foundation, has worked successfully for years to identify students from inner-city neighborhoods who have the determination and ability to succeed in a highly selective college.[10] The foundation has persuaded several dozen selective private colleges and universities to admit and give full scholarships to small groups (or "posses") of these students. Posse has gradually expanded its operations to include more cities and increase the number of colleges that agree to accept its students and give them the financial aid to finish. The vast majority have graduated. By now, a few other nonprofit organizations are also attempting to find low-income applicants and encourage them to apply to highly selective colleges.

Critics who urge very selective colleges to admit many more low-income applicants seem to assume that any students with reasonably good high school grades would succeed in a highly competitive college if only they were admitted. It is instructive, therefore, to take note of how the Posse Foundation goes about selecting the students who qualify for its programs. Posse does not simply choose students with good grades and board scores. In fact, the foundation does not pay much attention to grades and scores. It begins by asking inner-city high school teachers, guidance counselors, and principals to recommend juniors in their school who they believe have the character, resilience, ambition, and other personal qualities to flourish in a highly selective, competitive college. It then asks these students to take special tests that are devised to identify candidates who truly possess the qualities of initiative, leadership, and determination that Posse deems essential to success. The students selected attend weekend classes during their senior year in high school that prepare them to make the most of their college experience both in and outside the classroom. Finally, the students are sent to a selective college in small groups, or "posses," so that they can support each other in adjusting to their new and challenging environment. Approximately 90 percent do graduate. Some of them not only finish but also become student body presidents or achieve other positions of leadership. What Posse's success suggests, however, is that finding suitable students and preparing them to succeed is a good deal harder than simply persuading highly selective colleges to alter their admissions policies.

Supporting Posse students is not inexpensive. In addition to all-expenses-paid scholarships, the foundation needs a lot of money to locate, evaluate, and prepare inner-city students who have the perseverance and determination to succeed in selective colleges. Private institutions with ample endowments can help pay these costs by providing the necessary scholarships, but other colleges may lack the money to participate. Moreover, programs such as Posse's have concentrated their efforts on cities. Whether ways can be found to reach students living in smaller towns and rural communities, persuade them to apply, and prepare them to succeed remains to be seen.

To summarize, critics of current admissions policies have correctly identified several practices that are unfair and should be eliminated. It is unlikely, however, that removing these methods, by itself, will lead to significant increases in the number of low-income students admitted to elite colleges. Several of the dubious practices do not have as great an effect on admissions as critics tend to assume. Moreover, most of the students who would be next in line to fill the added vacancies if the needed reforms were adopted would probably look very much like the students already being admitted. This fact is not a reason to continue the objectionable practices. But it does suggest that making admissions procedures more fair will not do much by itself to gain the objective that critics hope to achieve. Added progress might be made if selective colleges gave a greater preference to students from low-income families, but only if these colleges can succeed in locating promising candidates for admission and persuading them to apply. Not all selective colleges can afford to undertake this expensive effort, however, and it remains unclear how many more low-income students would apply if they did so.

ARE MORE RADICAL PROPOSALS THE ANSWER?

To bring about a more substantial increase in the number of lower-income students admitted to selective colleges, several critics have suggested bolder remedies. Some readers may consider their proposals too radical to deserve detailed scrutiny.

Nevertheless, all the authors are respected scholars, and their ideas have received enough attention to warrant a careful analysis.

The late Lani Guinier, a Harvard Law professor, was an early critic of the way selective universities chose their students and was among the first to suggest a radical solution. She proposed that colleges and professional schools abandon their current admissions policies and instead choose their students by a lottery among all applicants meeting a set of minimum academic qualifications established by each institution. Her motive in doing so was to suggest a better alternative than an excessive reliance on standardized tests such as the SAT, which she felt were unreliable in predicting academic success and biased against Black students and other minority applicants.*

Guinier correctly pointed out that lotteries would provide a fairer way to give all academically qualified applicants an equal chance of being admitted to elite universities. Yet lotteries by themselves provide no guarantee that low-income students will participate. If few genuinely low-income students currently apply to highly selective colleges, why will larger numbers decide to enter a lottery?

Controversy is also bound to occur over how to define the qualifications to enter the lottery. High school grades alone seem unsatisfactory because they do not adjust for large differences in

*Guinier and Sturm, *Who's Qualified?* (2001). Guinier did not necessarily regard lotteries as either the best or the only alternative to standardized tests. Later she seemed to be most enthusiastic about the tests developed by the Posse Foundation to select Posse scholars to receive all-expenses-paid scholarships to selective four-year colleges. Posse's tests are ingenious and appear to work well in selecting scholarship winners from a limited group of candidates in a single city. They require trained evaluators and a lot of time to administer, however, and hence might not be practical for colleges and universities attempting to choose among many thousands of applicants scattered in cities and towns across the United States and abroad.

the significance of grades between highly selective high schools, such as Boston Latin School or Phillips Academy, and inner-city schools in Chicago or New Orleans. One obvious solution is to employ some standardized entrance exam, as in countries such as Japan or France. But tests of this kind will raise the same kind of objections as have arisen over the SAT and ACT exams.

Even if these problems can be surmounted, lottery systems will play havoc with existing methods of selecting students. Admissions officers at highly selective colleges attach great importance to their ability to craft an entering class that fits the special needs and characteristics of the college they serve. They try to make sure that they admit enough beefy linemen and fleet wide receivers to keep the football team competitive. They try to admit more students who express an interest in subjects such as history and literature that have suffered from declining enrollments in recent decades. They make an effort to favor applicants who seem likely to do well academically and make a significant contribution to society in their later lives. They try to assemble a diverse student body with members from different parts of the country, different races, different backgrounds, and special talents. They believe that they understand what kinds of students are most likely to thrive in their college and try to select applicants who display these characteristics.

The effort to match admissions with the particular needs and special nature of the college would be difficult or impossible under a lottery system.* This result may not trouble reformers

---

*Lottery advocates have suggested that students who meet special needs of selective colleges could be given two lottery tickets instead of one. Such an adjustment could be of some help but not enough to solve the problem. Football coaches will hardly believe that their needs will be met, nor will admissions officers be confident that the entering class will be well suited to the environment of their college.

who are single-minded in their determination to make the admissions process accept more minority or low-income students. But admissions officials will insist that something very valuable has been lost, and they are in a better position to make that judgment than most of their critics.*

An equally serious problem would arise under a lottery system from the inability of selective colleges to control their financial aid costs. If the lottery happened to yield too many needy students, a college might lack the money to give them the financial aid to remain and graduate. If too few low-income students survived the lottery, colleges would accomplish less than they otherwise might to further the purpose the lottery was designed to achieve.[11]

Faced with such uncertain outcomes, selective colleges would face an obvious dilemma in setting the minimum standards for allowing students to participate. If they tried to protect the academic qualifications of their student body as a whole by setting the qualifying grade averages and test scores at a high level, they might include too few minorities or low-income applicants to

---

*Some critics may believe that leading colleges and universities do not need to select their students with care because an elite degree by itself will give any graduate of reasonable ability the credential that guarantees an ample income in later life. This assumption seems highly implausible. Attending a highly selective university will probably improve a student's chances of graduating. At best, however, an elite degree will only help graduates obtain their first job. After that, employers will hardly be so naive as to keep promoting them on the strength of the college they attended. Success in a career depends on performance on the job, not on where one went to college. Perhaps proponents of a lottery system believe that the quality of education at elite institutions is so much better than that of other colleges and universities that graduates admitted by lottery will have the same success in later life as students chosen in the current manner. Much as I would like to believe this argument, I know of no evidence that supports it and much evidence that contradicts it.

achieve a suitably diverse class. If they set the qualifying requirements much lower to provide a more diverse pool, they would depress the academic qualifications of their entering students well below their current levels.

Most selective colleges would probably choose to set the qualifications for the lottery at a high level rather than depress them enough to run the risk of having to admit more low-income students than they can afford or diminish the academic quality of their entire class. Colleges that are not as wealthy as the most selective institutions might raise the qualifications high enough to avoid any possibility of having to enroll more needy students than they could afford. Thus, a lottery could have the ironic result of *reducing* rather than increasing the number of low-income and minority students admitted to selective institutions.

The many practical problems created by introducing a lottery are sufficient to dim the prospects for enacting such a system into law. The disruption of intercollegiate athletics would be enough by itself to doom the proposal in many state legislatures where elected representatives, along with many of their constituents, set great store by the success of their football and basketball teams. The financial hazards created by such a process and its destructive effect on selecting a class that meets the various legitimate needs of the colleges involved would undoubtedly provoke determined opposition from a wide variety of academic leaders.

Another Harvard professor, Michael Sandel, has also proposed a lottery among all applicants possessing the minimum qualifications that the university considers essential to succeed and flourish academically.[12] As a result, his proposal suffers from most of the same difficulties as Guinier's. What Sandel is trying to accomplish, however, is not just to make access to college fairer but to undermine the very system of meritocracy that the admissions policies of selective universities tend to embrace. As it is, he believes, meritocracy has exacerbated differences in attitude between selective college graduates and other people by giving the former an unhealthy sense of superiority while providing another reason for the latter to feel inferior and disrespected.

Sandel recommends a lottery scheme as a way to diminish the corrosive sense of superiority. If lotteries were required, students in selective colleges could no longer regard themselves as special because their talents, virtues, and other personal qualities have been recognized as outstanding in an exacting competition against thousands of other candidates for admission. Instead, they would merely be students who were lucky enough to win a lottery.

It is most unlikely, however, that meritocracy and its problems can be vanquished so easily. Students attending elite colleges would still gain the distinction of being qualified intellectually to participate in the lottery of an elite university. They would still have the benefit of what many people believe to be an exceptional undergraduate education. Graduates who have received high grades from a leading college will still be preferred by many employers and will receive the best job offers. Moreover, even if a lottery managed to eliminate the higher status and the feeling of superiority given to students accepted to top-ranked colleges, employers would presumably find other meritocratic ways to identify the graduates they most wished to hire. Thus, Sandel would deprive selective colleges of their freedom to choose the entering class they consider most appropriate in order to pursue what would almost certainly prove to be a fruitless effort to achieve a more just and harmonious society.

David Kirp from the Berkeley campus of the University of California published an article on the opinion page of the *New York Times* proposing a much simpler way to increase opportunity for low-income students without encountering the problems of a lottery.[13] What elite institutions such as Yale and Stanford could do, according to Kirp, is open a branch campus in another part of the country that would be largely devoted to educating students from financially deprived households and neighborhoods. Kirp assumes that a degree from the new satellite of a highly selective university would provide low-income graduates with the same later-life advantages enjoyed by students who studied at its traditional campus.

If this assumption were correct, students who currently graduate with a BA degree from Harvard's Extension School would enjoy the same advantages as graduates from Harvard College. This is clearly not the case. Rightly or wrongly, the advantages that accrue from earning a traditional Harvard BA are not available to anyone with a Harvard diploma. They are contingent on two essential factors: that Harvard College graduates were chosen from a huge number of applicants, most of whom had excellent academic credentials, and that they received a very expensive education taught by a faculty of renowned scientists and scholars. Thus, for Kirp's proposal to succeed, the satellite college created by an elite university would have to assemble a similarly talented faculty with a similarly competitive admissions process and a sufficiently generous program of financial aid to attract many thousands of low-income applicants every year. The cost of developing such a faculty with the laboratories, libraries, and graduate programs that such professors would demand, together with the expense of providing the students with the necessary financial aid, would require enormous amounts of money and take many years to assemble. The likelihood that even the wealthiest university would adopt such a costly proposal is therefore close to zero.

A faculty member from Yale Law School, Daniel Markovits, has advanced still another bold proposal to increase the number of students from lower-income families who are admitted to highly selective universities.[14] Like Sandel, Markovits is strongly opposed to meritocracy, at least in its present form. Unlike Sandel, however, he does not simply deplore the lack of opportunities given to lower-income students. Nor does he assert a tendency for graduates from elite universities to consider themselves superior and for those less fortunate to feel resentful and disrespected. What he particularly dislikes is the disappearance of middle-class manufacturing jobs that once gave stability to many communities and opportunities for secure employment with decent wages, benefits, and steadily growing incomes for millions of Americans.

Markovits also marshals much supporting evidence to show that successful meritocrats pay a great price for their extravagant financial rewards. He describes in detail the seventy-hour workweeks, the frequent travel, the resulting problems of alcohol, drugs, suicide, and broken marriages accompanied by the constant threat of losing one's lucrative place in a relentlessly competitive and insecure meritocracy. In addition, he points out, the rich feel obliged to undergo the costly and time-consuming effort of preparing their children to achieve financial success by giving them the best, most expensive education and helping them build the kind of résumés necessary to gain admission to elite colleges and professional schools.

According to Markovits, therefore, the current meritocratic system leaves everyone dissatisfied. Those who are truly successful are extravagantly paid but at the heavy cost of being overworked and insecure, while everyone else suffers from an economy that no longer offers them enough of those middle-class jobs that used to guarantee secure employment and steadily growing paychecks.

To overcome these conditions, Markovits does not dwell on reforming the current admissions process or recommend the use of lotteries. His proposal is simpler but equally drastic. He recommends that each selective university be required to admit at least half of every entering class from the bottom two-thirds of the income scale or else forfeit its exemptions from taxes on income, property, endowment earnings, and donations. Since no leading universities can afford to do without these tax advantages, they will have no choice but to accept the quota.

This proposal would clearly expand the opportunities for students from lower-income families to enter the best-known universities. Interestingly, however, Markovits does not favor reducing the number of students from families in the highest income brackets who attend these institutions. Instead, like Kirp, he would prefer to have leading universities fill their quota of lower-income students by expanding the size of their student bodies, perhaps with the help of financial assistance from the federal government to reduce the added expense of having to educate a much larger student body.

To increase the number of middle-class jobs, Markovits advocates an effort by the government to change the payroll tax to encourage the creation of reasonably well-paid jobs, such as nurse practitioners who would be allowed to perform the more routine functions now provided by MDs and legal assistants who could carry out the many simple legal tasks that do not require fully trained lawyers. In this way, Markovits hopes to improve the lives of those who cannot reap the rewards of meritocratic success by offering them the kinds of relatively secure, decently paid middle-class jobs whose disappearance he deplores. Meanwhile, he predicts that the wealthy elites will eventually see the folly of their ways and accept lower incomes in order to live a less hectic and insecure existence.

This deceptively simple remedy contains a host of serious problems. To begin with, the cost to leading universities would be enormous, whether they have to spend far more on financial aid by enrolling half of their existing classes from the bottom two-thirds of the income scale or assume the even greater cost of expanding their size to admit a much larger student body. Like many critics, Markovits brushes this problem aside, asserting that the large endowments of the most prominent institutions can easily take care of any added costs. In doing so, he does not come to grips with the full amount of the added costs, ignores the fact that not all highly selective universities have huge endowments, and fails to recognize that most of the money in every endowment is restricted to particular purposes specified by the donor that the university is legally bound to respect.[15]

Many of the changes that Markovits plans to bring about through his reforms seem equally problematic. He hopes to replenish the number of stable, middle-income jobs by simply changing the payroll tax to make such jobs less expensive for employers while increasing the cost of hiring highly educated, lavishly paid employees. He also hopes that the wealthy, highly educated elites will tire of being overworked and insecure and will welcome a return to the conditions of the 1950s and 1960s, when the incomes of law firm partners, CEOs, and other captains of finance were much lower but their lives were much less hectic and insecure.

Whether and when these changes might come about seems far less obvious than Markovits suggests. One is reminded of John Maynard Keynes's prediction in 1930 that in a few generations a growing economy would provide sufficient incomes to allow everyone to work much less and use their added leisure time to enjoy the finer things of life. Almost a century has passed, yet the highest-paid Americans are working harder than ever. Meanwhile, although the gross national product has greatly increased, there are still many homeless people, children who go hungry, adults without health care, and single mothers who must find jobs to feed their families.[16]

Finally, in addition to their other problems, all the drastic remedies discussed are susceptible to the kinds of unforeseen consequences that often result from enacting sweeping proposals unaccompanied by adequate evidence and careful analysis of their effects. Such remedies are especially dangerous in considering how to regulate our most selective universities. Whatever their faults, these universities do much good work. Their hospitals rank among the finest in the quality of care they offer. Their faculties have helped make America preeminent in basic research and produced discoveries that have contributed enormously to the growth of our economy. Any remedy that threatens to alter these institutions substantially should be adopted only after far more careful thought and supporting evidence than any of the drastic reforms just described have received.

THE BOTTOM LINE

The weaknesses and dangers associated with the remedies just discussed do not remove the need to improve the existing methods for admitting students to elite universities. Critics rightly argue that selective universities can hardly insist on the importance of allowing them to choose the applicants with the greatest promise when they continue to offer advantages to the children of wealthy parents and other favored groups that have little to do with their ability to contribute to society. These current practices may offer modest financial gains to their universities, but they conflict with more important public purposes that our leading colleges and universities ought to serve. The additional gifts from grateful parents may be essential for some colleges that are struggling to survive, but that is hardly a valid excuse for our highly selective universities. These favored institutions should consequently abandon their questionable admissions practices as soon as possible, if only to increase the confidence of the public and avoid the risk of inviting government regulation.

As this book was about to be printed, Raj Chetty and two of his colleagues published a new report identifying the career advantages for students who attend an elite private university and revealing how much of a preference admissions officers give to applicants who are legacies, recruited athletes, or seniors from a private preparatory school.[17] These findings provide convincing empirical support for reducing or eliminating these preferences in order to increase the fairness of the admissions process and the economic diversity of the entering class.

At the same time, it is not at all clear that ending these preferences would do very much to increase the admission of low-income applicants. If we compare the makeup of Harvard's entering class with that of MIT, which does not employ the preferences analyzed by Chetty, MIT enrolls fewer students from families with incomes in the top 1 percent—or the top 5, 10, or 20 percent, for that matter. Nevertheless, both colleges admit the same percentage of students receiving federal Pell Grants, almost all of which go to students from low-income families earning $50,000 or less per year. In order to substantially increase the number of low-income students, therefore, admissions offices will probably need to give these applicants a greater boost in the admissions process than they are already receiving. Even this step will not succeed unless elite colleges manage to locate enough qualified low-income students and persuade them to apply. In short, even if selected universities stopped their suspect practices, as I believe they should, few low-income students are likely to be next in line to take the places thereby vacated. As Sandy Baum and Michael McPherson conclude in their detailed study of the subject, "Until we get serious about reducing the substantial inequalities in the lives of children, we should anticipate only limited success in making college success more equal."[18] Important built-in advantages for the well-to-do will remain, such as the ability to pay for child care and quality preschool education, to live in safe neighborhoods, and to have their children attend better schools than those available to most sons and daughters of low-income parents. As long as these differences remain, admissions officers will have limited success in trying to identify promising low-income students and persuading them to apply.

These arguments may not satisfy critics who have little trust in the motives or the judgment of elite universities and continue to urge the admission of more and more students from low-income families. Although their goal is admirable, the remedies they propose threaten to do greater damage than any good they might do. In the end, the effort to provide greater equality of opportunity must be fought on many fronts, including providing better and more universal preschool education, reducing the number of children who grow up in poverty, narrowing the gap in quality between schools in poor and wealthy communities, strengthening labor unions, mending the safety net to protect the less fortunate from the hazards of life, improving conditions in low-income neighborhoods, and much else. Many of these reforms are hard to bring about politically and will cost a great deal of money. But that is no reason for pretending that the opportunities for children from low-income families can be greatly improved by simply changing the admissions procedures of a few dozen highly selective colleges and universities.

CHAPTER 4

Student Protests and the Role of Elite Universities in Combating Evil and Injustice in the World

M Y TWENTY YEARS AT HARVARD WERE MARKED BY repeated student demands regarding the role that the University should play in responding to evils and injustices in the outside world. Shortly before I took office, students and some faculty members as well had urged Harvard to declare its opposition to the Vietnam War. These pleas, however, soon subsided and did not reappear thereafter, perhaps because most students and faculty believed that the University administration might inhibit freedom of thought if it purported to speak for the entire institution on controversial issues. There were other attempts in the 1960s to have the University boycott goods produced by companies engaged in questionable activities, such as the campaign to have the college stop buying lettuce from growers in California who resisted the efforts of Cesar Chavez to organize migrant farmworkers. The "lettuce campaign" ended successfully when the administrative vice president suddenly announced that the University would henceforth buy only union produce. For reasons unknown to me, boycotts of this kind had also largely disappeared by the time I took office.

Another kind of protest, however, arose during my first year and continued nearly every spring for the rest of my presidency. The underlying cause was Harvard's ownership of stock in companies doing business in countries with unjust and repressive policies. The first of these disputes culminated in a ten-day student occupation of Massachusetts Hall, where I and my vice presidents had our offices, to protest the University's investment in a company that drilled and refined oil in Angola, then a colony under the harsh regime of Portugal. I refused to discuss the matter as long as the students continued to occupy the building on the grounds that the University should never make policy decisions in response to improper and disruptive pressure tactics. After ten days, the students withdrew as suddenly as they had come, leaving the building neater and cleaner than it had been when they entered. I remember no further building occupations during my presidency.

When Portugal withdrew from Angola not long thereafter, students turned for the next sixteen years to a campaign to persuade Harvard to divest its holdings in companies doing business in South Africa under its cruel and oppressive apartheid regime. I resisted these demands throughout this entire period and doubtless earned the displeasure of many students and their allies as a result.

CONTRASTING VIEWS ABOUT PROTESTS OVER THE USE OF UNIVERSITY INVESTMENTS

Why did I resist the student demands to divest the stock of companies operating in South Africa? Surely not because I had any sympathy for apartheid, a thoroughly heartless and inhumane policy. Nor was I opposed to divestment in all cases.

On one occasion, I even directed our investment managers to sell all our holdings in tobacco companies, although I had not received any student demands to do so. For a long time, I had naively believed that since the risks of smoking had been widely publicized, those who still smoked must have decided that the pleasures of tobacco outweighed the dangers to their health. A chance conversation with my wife, however, alerted me to the fact that the tobacco companies were compensating for the decline in the number of adult smokers by targeting teenagers and populations in poor countries where no warning labels were required, and millions of people could not read them in any event. I realized then that my reasons for retaining these investments were untenable. By chance, the Harvard Corporation was meeting that morning. I explained my change of mind to the members, and the order to sell our tobacco stocks was communicated shortly before noon.

To me, selling tobacco stocks was not done to bring pressure on the companies involved to stop producing cigarettes. Such an effort would have been fruitless. I simply believed that Harvard should not make money from investing in companies whose product caused great harm to millions of people while offering virtually no redeeming benefit.

Selling stock in all companies doing business in South Africa struck me as an entirely different matter. The corporations involved were not primarily engaged in selling products that were intrinsically harmful and had little or no redeeming value. Instead, the companies were selling respectable products in many different countries, and their activity in South Africa was typically only a tiny part of their total operation. As a result, there was no reason to believe that the business of these companies was inherently immoral. In fact, the companies involved were not the real target. Rather, the aim of the protesting students in seeking to have these companies cease their operations in South Africa was to punish the government for its apartheid program and treat it as a pariah state so that it would abandon its cruel and inhumane policy.

I had grave reservations about using the Harvard endowment as a weapon to further the policy goals favored by the University. In my mind, the appropriate way for a university to influence public policy was through its research and the arguments publicly expressed by its professors. If students wished to make their voices heard, they should sign a petition, not bring pressure to bear on the president and trustees to sell the University's stock. Since the reasons for my position may not be immediately obvious, they require a more careful examination.

Protests of this kind have not disappeared, nor are they unique to Harvard. They have erupted from time to time at other universities as well. Most of these institutions are elites because these are the universities with large enough endowments and sufficient reputations that their decision to divest will be newsworthy and hence may help persuade the corporations involved to alter their behavior.

In thinking about this subject, it is useful to begin by trying to understand the reasons why protesting students and university leaders, all of whom are well-intentioned, are often unable to resolve their differences amicably. Contrary to what some students may believe, there is rarely any disagreement over the underlying cause for which the students are fighting. In my time, both sides agreed that apartheid was a cruel, inhumane policy that was entirely unjustified. Both sides today understand that climate change is a terrible danger and that human actions, especially those that contribute to carbon emissions, are chiefly responsible for the problem.

I should also make clear that I find nothing wrong with students proposing changes in the policies of their university. Quite the contrary. In the late 1980s, a group of students from several faculties in the University sent me a detailed set of proposals for changing existing practices in order to reduce pollution. When the students arrived in my office to discuss their recommendations, I opened the meeting by telling them that I had read their paper carefully and agreed with all of their suggestions and that I would proceed immediately to have them implemented. Thus, my disagreement with divestment was not that students were meddling with the administration of the University. I was simply not persuaded that selling stock to influence public policy was a sound course of action for the University to pursue.

The argument over fossil fuels and other disputes like it results in large part from a difference in the way each side looks at the use of divestment to influence corporate behavior. For students engaged in such a protest, the effort to bring about the sale of fossil fuel stock (or the stock of other companies) stems from a strong and commendable desire by the students involved to do something tangible to improve the world instead of merely enjoying a privileged life in a leading university. The chance to contribute in this way is a deeply satisfying opportunity for the participants that is not to be given up lightly. It is the product of a sentiment that almost everyone will applaud and an expression of social responsibility that college presidents frequently emphasize in welcoming entering freshmen and exhorting departing seniors.

While respecting students' motives, however, college presidents view demands to divest stock very differently from the way the protest leaders and their followers do. The students are wholly preoccupied with the particular cause for which they are fighting, but presidents must take account of a wider set of consequences that could follow from embarking on a policy of selling stock to achieve political or social goals.

The concerns that weigh on the minds of most presidents stem from the realization that a great many companies are likely to be engaged in some activity that others might criticize on ethical or social policy grounds. With respect to climate change alone, students could protest not only against the major oil producers but also against the firms that sell them machinery, or that participate in building pipelines and tankers, or that manufacture products that emit large quantities of carbon dioxide, such as cars, trucks, and airplanes.

Many issues other than climate change can also lead to demands for divestment. Already, student groups have urged the sale of stock in companies that help build or operate prisons. Selling the shares of companies that make assault rifles or that repeatedly violate the law in their effort to discourage unionization are among the many other plausible possibilities for divestment demands. Some of these protests may give rise to highly divisive conflicts within the university itself. For example, one student group has urged Harvard to divest the stock of companies doing business in Israel to protest Israeli policies toward Palestinians in Gaza and the West Bank. This issue has already led to passionate disagreements on a number of campuses among students, alumni, and members of the faculty.

For these reasons, the cost of selling stock in companies for social or political purposes can trouble the university administration on financial grounds. Those who urge divestment from fossil fuel companies typically argue that selling the shares of these few firms will hardly have much impact on a university's endowment and may even turn out to be a wise investment decision. College officials, however, will almost certainly be aware that establishing a precedent for divesting for ethical or policy reasons could eventually lead to selling the stock of many more than a few corporations. As student demands extend to more and more companies, the financial consequences are bound eventually to lower the performance of the endowment and hence affect the amount of money the university can spend on the salaries of faculty and staff, the financial aid given to students, and the operation of existing educational programs. Since college presidents have a fiduciary responsibility to the students, faculty, and administrative employees, they will hardly be persuaded by arguments that selling the stock of a few fossil fuel companies will have no appreciable effect on endowment income.

Endowment income is not the only interest of the university that presidents may seek to defend. One intangible value that is even more important to universities is the preservation of academic freedom—the right of individual professors and students to express their thoughts and beliefs without fear of penalties of any sort, even if their opinions are contrary to those of campus officials. It is concern for this freedom that has helped persuade many universities to resist making official declarations of the institution's position on matters of politics and public policy other than those directly affecting higher education, such as the government's financial aid proposals.

Students may not think that divestment decisions made on ethical or policy grounds could have any effect on the willingness of professors to speak their minds. That may be true with respect to the tenured faculty. But many instructors may not feel as secure from such pressures as full professors. Junior faculty members hoping to receive tenure and adjunct faculty on year-to-year appointments might hesitate to openly support policies contradicting a widely publicized position of the university on selling the stock of companies operating in Israel or some other controversial issue.

Academic leaders may perceive still another danger that could result from using endowments to influence corporate behavior on moral or policy grounds. Universities have traditionally enjoyed considerable autonomy in making academic decisions such as what to teach and whom to hire as professors or admit as students. Such freedom is extremely important for the quality of academic institutions and should be guarded with great care. As several commentators have pointed out in analyzing the reasons for the success of our elite universities, an important contributing factor has been their autonomy from government control.[1] Once a university enters the political arena by using its investments as a weapon to influence the behavior of companies and the policies of governments, it will invite interference from external sources. The government of Texas has already banned Goldman Sachs and JPMorgan Chase from handling state bond sales "because of their support for gun safety regulations and alternative energy." Similar retribution could await universities that use divestment to influence corporate policies.[2]

Harvard and other leading universities are not immune from retaliatory pressures of this kind. In fact, they are especially vulnerable because of their wealth and reputation and because the views expressed by their professors are often upsetting to powerful legislators and other public officials. Already, amid the ideological battles and culture wars of contemporary politics, government officials have begun to interfere in unprecedented ways with the educational policies of universities. (See chapters 6 and 11.) In today's contentious environment, universities that use their investments to promote their views on matters of social policy could provoke political officials to intervene even more frequently in academic affairs.*

Finally, underlying all the arguments just summarized is a serious doubt on the part of university officials that selling stock will have any effect on corporate behavior. It is entirely possible that divestment will simply transfer shares to other investors who have no qualms about holding the stock of fossil fuel companies, gun makers, or any other companies with favorable financial prospects. If so, a more effective course of action for universities might be to vote for shareholder resolutions to persuade companies to change their behavior in particular ways. For example, in the case of fossil fuels, resolutions might call on management to adopt a different policy by spending less on prospecting for new sources of oil and more on research to promote alternative sources of energy. In contrast, students who simply demand divestment often suggest no practical course of action that companies could conceivably accept.

Protesters scoff at the idea of shareholder resolutions, arguing that they are bound to be ineffective. They undoubtedly have a point. Resolutions urging companies to take socially responsible

---

*It is true that universities already act collectively in voting on shareholder resolutions that may include measures involving controversial issues of public policy. In doing so, however, universities are acting pursuant to the methods of corporate governance established by law. The votes that universities cast in particular cases rarely attract public attention or serve any purpose other than that envisaged by the law. In contrast, efforts to have major universities divest are initiated because they will attract attention and generate publicity that will increase the pressure on the corporations involved to change their policy in the way students desire. The fact that divestment is unusual and that it is primarily a moral judgment against the corporation gives it whatever power it possesses to sway public opinion and makes it especially likely to arouse resentment from the corporations involved and from other outsiders.

actions seldom succeed, at least immediately, although one such campaign has forced a major oil company to appoint three environmentally friendly representatives to its board of directors. Students insist, therefore, that only divestment is strong enough medicine to attract the attention of the media and generate pressure to induce companies to change their ways. Harvard students who are engaged in protests seem especially likely to believe that a decision by the University to divest will be consequential. "It will change the conversation about fossil fuels," one student was quoted as saying. I can only reply that my twenty-one years as president left me far less sanguine about the extent of Harvard's influence.

In the end, there is little hard evidence one way or the other on the effects of selling stock. Helen Suzman, the gallant woman who was the sole outspoken opponent of apartheid in the South African Parliament, where she repeatedly expressed her opposition at some personal risk, twice urged me not to divest, insisting that it would only harden the determination of the Afrikaners to maintain the status quo. On the other hand, proponents of divestment will respond by pointing to the subsequent decision by the South African government to abandon apartheid altogether. In fact, however, no one really knows what finally led Prime Minister F. W. de Klerk and his Afrikaner followers to change their minds and abandon that singularly cruel and inhumane policy.

In ultimately deciding against the use of divestment to achieve social policy objectives, I was aware that many people might conclude that Harvard was simply choosing to place money ahead of justice and ethical principles. As a result, I went to considerable lengths to try to counteract this impression. On two separate occasions, I explained the reasons for my decision in an open letter, much as I have in the preceding pages, and had this paper delivered to every student and published for the entire University.

In addition, to dispel any notion that the University was merely defending the profits it received from the South African operations of companies in our investment portfolio, I initiated a scholarship program to bring several Black South African students to Harvard annually for a year's study. In the end, every one of these students returned to South Africa instead of seeking asylum in the United States, and several assumed positions of leadership. The money devoted to this program surely exceeded any profits Harvard received from business done in South Africa.

I have no way of knowing what effect my efforts had on the attitudes of our students toward the University. Interestingly, several leaders of the student protests have written unsolicited letters to me many years later telling me that they have come to understand my arguments much better after leaving Harvard. Admittedly, these are only straws in the wind and hardly support any general conclusions. What I continue to believe, however, is that disputes over the ethics of university investment policies are inescapably a part of students' moral education and need to be treated as such by presidents.

CURRENT REFLECTIONS

Now that thirty years and more have elapsed since I left office, I recognize that the world has moved on and attitudes toward divestment have changed. A substantial number of elite universities, including Harvard, Yale, and Stanford, have embraced some form of environmentally responsible investing and have sold or agreed to sell all or part of their investments in fossil fuels. Several pension plans and other funds are also employing socially responsible investing that avoids holding stock in companies that are engaged in activities that contribute to global warming.

Notwithstanding these later developments, I remain a skeptic with respect to the use of divestment as a means of persuading companies to change their behavior. I still believe that selling stock is an ineffective way to try to change corporate policies. Although shareholder resolutions may be no more effective, at least they make clear to fossil fuel companies exactly what they are being urged to do. I continue to fear that issuing official university positions on matters of social, economic, or industrial policy may inhibit the willingness of vulnerable members of the university community to express a contrary opinion. Most of all, I worry that if leaders and trustees of elite institutions try to influence policy by using their endowments and prestige to advance social goals, they will provoke conservative officials to intervene more often in the academic affairs of leading universities. That risk is considerably greater than it was when I was president.

For all these reasons, I continue to believe that sending petitions signed by individual students, faculty, or employees and informing public opinion by publishing the arguments and research from individual members of the faculty are the most appropriate ways in which universities can help shape the opinions of government officials, corporations, and the public as a whole. At the same time, I recognize that there are many people who disagree with my position, and I respect their opinions. I am even willing to concede that they may possibly be right. After all, divestment is not resolvable by logic alone. It is a matter of judgment. In issues of this kind, reasonable people may differ, and no one can be certain who is right or wrong.

If universities do decide to embrace divestment as a means of supporting policy goals, the question remains how divestment decisions should be made. On most campuses, such proposals have typically been initiated by ad hoc groups of students who seek to convince the president or trustees (or both) to sell certain investments for moral or public policy reasons. If their arguments do not prevail, the students try to persuade political allies to join their cause, such as other students or members of the faculty. They may enlist alumni to run for election to the board of trustees. Not infrequently, they engage in some sort of disruptive activity to call attention to their cause and exert more pressure on the university administration.

This method of proceeding has many disadvantages. It leads activist groups to use disruptive tactics to force the administration to divest. It also puts the entire weight of decision making on the shoulders of one person, the president. This burden can be heavy, especially in times like the present when several different student groups may be formed simultaneously, each with its own set of demands.

Presidents already have too little time to concentrate on matters of research and education that are the primary functions of the institution. Moreover, while these leaders are chosen on the basis of their academic judgment and experience, they are by no means experts in matters of public policy. At Harvard, for example, though the University has had distinguished presidents, such as Charles W. Eliot and A. Lawrence Lowell, their judgments on issues such as immigration, trade unions, eugenics, anti-Semitism, and race hardly seem wise in retrospect.

All things considered, then, if universities choose to embrace socially responsible investing, they will be well-advised to create a more structured and broadly based process for making controversial decisions. Although no one procedure may be ideally suited to all universities, several features seem appropriate for most. First of all, proposals to divest the stock of particular companies should not go immediately to the president. Instead, they should initially be submitted to a representative committee created to collect the relevant arguments and information and decide whether divestment is appropriate.

The composition of the committee and the methods for choosing its members may vary from one university to another, but it should ideally include representatives from all the main constituent groups: the faculty, the alumni, the students, and the administration. To gain the necessary confidence and respect, members other than the representatives of the administration should be chosen not by the president but by the established groups representing each constituency—for example, the faculty senate or some similar body, the alumni organization or a vote of the alumni, and the student government.

Since the trustees have been given final authority over the policies of universities, the decisions of the committee will have to be approved by the board. As a practical matter, however, trustees will be very reluctant to overrule the recommendation of such a committee, save in exceptional cases.

A procedure like the one just described will not remove all the possible risks and disadvantages of having universities embark on a policy of passing judgment on the policies and practices of corporations in a university's portfolio. The positions arrived at in this fashion may still inhibit the free speech of vulnerable members of the faculty or invite intervention by government officials. At the same time, if divestment decisions are made by a procedure such as the one recommended here, it is likely that they will at least gain respect as a considered and legitimate expression of the institution's judgment.

CHAPTER 5

Reparations

The Bitter Legacy of Slavery and an Attempt to Repair the Damage

TWO HUNDRED AND FIFTY YEARS OF SLAVERY IN America followed by the lamentable practice of discrimination and injustice during the century after the Civil War hover like a dark cloud over the history of the United States, blurring our image of America as a shining "city on a hill" and an example to the world of freedom and democracy. As historians come to grips with this shameful record, Black leaders and intellectuals have raised the issue of reparations and other acts of contrition to help repair the damage to the lives of Black Americans.

This question has a long history. In the aftermath of Lincoln's Emancipation Proclamation, political leaders began to consider what might be done to give former slaves a decent start now that they were fully able to begin their life as free citizens. Promises were made, notably a gift of forty acres and a mule for each slave family. In the end, however, these promises were not kept, and

Blacks were left on their own to make what they could of their new freedom. What followed was a now-familiar story of brutal suppression in the South marked by lynchings, mob violence, systematic denial of adequate education, and a proliferation of discriminatory practices throughout the rest of the country that excluded Blacks from all manner of opportunities and advantages enjoyed by Whites. The harm done by centuries of slavery, discrimination, and exclusion has given rise to much debate over whether and how to repay the victims of these deplorable practices and their descendants or atone in other ways for the injuries inflicted.

In addition to the individuals and institutions that participated in acts of injustice or discrimination, the entire White population has arguably benefited from the lingering effects of the many practices that have exploited the labor of Black Americans and hindered them from competing on equal terms for jobs and other benefits available to most citizens. For that reason, some may believe that all Whites should feel an obligation not only to avoid contributing to further discrimination but to atone for the advantage they have gained from centuries of discrimination that have handicapped Blacks in competing against Whites for advancement and prosperity.

THE HISTORY OF REPARATIONS

The obvious way to compensate for past injustices of this kind would be through measures by the government. Efforts to obtain such compensation, however, have not been fruitful. A number of lawsuits have been brought to secure damages for some of the most flagrant acts of violence and oppression, such as the Tulsa Massacre of 1921. Almost all these efforts failed for a variety of reasons. Judges ruled either that the statute of limitations had elapsed, or that witnesses to the injustice were no longer alive, or that those who brought suit had no standing since they had not themselves suffered injury.

Attempts to secure redress from the legislature were similarly unsuccessful. In two cases of this kind Congress did provide compensation for government actions that were later found to be unjust: once for Japanese families interned during World War II and once for land in Alaska taken from Native Americans in violation of a treaty. In both instances, the money awarded was not intended as full compensation for the losses involved but was, rather, a way of expressing recognition for the injustice done. Reparations for slavery have never received even this much sympathy from Congress, although a few states and municipalities have recently begun to consider the possibility seriously.

Opponents have used a variety of arguments to explain their views. Senator Mitch McConnell has pointed out that all those responsible for slavery are dead and cannot be made to pay for their sins. Others maintain that reparations will exacerbate rather than alleviate racial tensions. Still others argue that much recent social legislation, such as Lyndon Johnson's Great Society initiative and a host of programs for low-income Americans costing many billions of dollars, including food stamps and welfare, disproportionately assist Black Americans and hence help compensate for past injustices. A few opponents have even argued that the Civil War, with its massive loss of life, was atonement enough for slavery.

THE CAMPAIGN FOR REPARATIONS
FROM ELITE UNIVERSITIES

Since Black claimants have failed to obtain compensation through the courts or the legislature, they have increasingly looked to private institutions to acknowledge their ties to slavery and provide reparations.[1] Elite universities are a natural target for such efforts.

Most of them were founded decades before the abolition of slavery and were complicit in various ways with the use of slaves. Many are among the wealthiest universities and so have ample resources for paying reparations. Not least, the nature of these institutions makes them unusually sympathetic to campaigns for social justice. Black students and faculty are natural supporters, and many of their White classmates are willing allies. White faculty members are predominantly liberal in their attitudes toward politics and social justice and may join in calling for an accounting. By now, several universities have conducted studies of their past involvement with slavery, acknowledged these ties and made them public, and established funds to be used in various ways to atone for these injustices.

THE HARVARD REPORT

In 2022 Harvard University issued a detailed report prepared by a faculty committee identifying the University's involvement with race from colonial times to the present day.[2] The University immediately responded by establishing a $100 million fund to be used for a variety of purposes, including compensation for descendants of slaves who were owned by Harvard presidents, faculty, and other University officials; furthering the education of Blacks and Native Americans; and engaging in cooperative programs with historically Black universities and local public schools. The Harvard report is worth examining carefully since the issues it raises are common to most of the attempts by large universities to come to terms with their past involvement with slavery and the many subsequent decades of widespread exclusion and discrimination.

The report itself consists chiefly of a meticulous compilation of the University's connections to slavery and its involvement with racial discrimination during the century following Lincoln's Emancipation Proclamation. It contains a wealth of relevant information about the many individuals associated with Harvard who owned slaves, and the various donations the University received in the eighteenth and nineteenth centuries from wealthy New Englanders who made their fortunes from the use of slaves on plantations in the West Indies or from ships that carried slaves or goods produced with slave labor from the Caribbean to markets in the United States.

Following the Civil War, Harvard continued to receive donations from wealthy mill owners whose businesses were built on goods made of cotton produced in the West Indies with slave labor. In addition, several of the University's professors in the nineteenth century, including the noted biologist Louis Agassiz, did extensive research attempting to prove that Blacks were an inferior race, an opinion shared by many others, including Stanford's president David Starr Jordan. From 1870 to the 1960s, Harvard College admitted a few Black students (an average of three per year), but the University made no special efforts to recruit them and sometimes forbade their living in student residence halls because of the opposition of White classmates.

The report does not deal exclusively with acts of exploitation and discrimination. The authors make numerous references to faculty members and students, Black and White, who strongly opposed slavery and racial discrimination. Toward the end of its account, the report devotes a page to the efforts of the University since the 1960s to enroll more Black students and to defend its methods for achieving racial diversity when they were attacked in the federal courts.

THE QUESTION OF MORAL RESPONSIBILITY

The bulk of the Harvard report proceeds in scholarly fashion to present the known facts without attempting to pass judgment on the behavior it describes. In the section titled "Recommendations," however, the authors issue a sweeping verdict on Harvard's moral responsibility for the many ties to slavery and discrimination described in the previous pages. As the report puts it: "Each of these forms of culpability—direct participation, financial ties, intellectual leadership, and discrimination—applies to Harvard. . . . And the responsibility for involvement with slavery is shared across the institution—by presidents, fellows of the Corporation, overseers, faculty, staff, donors, students, and namesakes memorialized all over campus."[3] Absent from the report is any effort to justify this all-encompassing definition of Harvard's culpability by explaining why the University should be held responsible for each of the many different connections with slavery and prejudice that the committee has so diligently catalogued.

The injustices inflicted by slavery and racial discrimination are so cruel and inhumane that any attempt to argue over the precise extent of Harvard's moral responsibility may strike some readers as petty and beside the point. Yet it is worth remembering that today's leaders and faculty may be judged some day for how they used the powers and duties entrusted to them. They will feel rudely treated if they are summarily found to be morally responsible without any attempt to explain the reasons why they should be found culpable. Other universities may also look to this widely publicized report in considering their own responsibility for racial injustice. If so, they will find little enlightenment, even though Harvard's moral responsibility for a number of the activities described in the report is open to serious question.

For example, the report finds that at least seventy-nine slaves can be identified as having been owned by presidents, faculty members, or trustees. Without question, Harvard should be held to account for any use of slaves to carry out functions of the University, such as building its residence halls or preparing food for the students. But it is much less clear that Harvard as an institution should have even been aware of, let alone been held responsible for, the domestic servants acquired by faculty members for their own private use. It is even less obvious that the University should be held accountable for the use of slaves by its Overseers, since Overseers were not chosen by Harvard before 1870 but were appointed by the Massachusetts legislature.

Another debatable issue is whether universities should be condemned for accepting gifts from donors such as Isaac Royall, who funded the first professorship at Harvard Law School in the nineteenth century after making a fortune from plantations in the West Indies that used slave labor. Is it fair to blame universities for accepting a gift before the donor's conduct has been clearly judged by society to be unlawful or immoral? For example, should Stanford University be faulted for accepting Leland Stanford's founding gift because he had brutally exploited many thousands of Chinese workers and wrested so much land from Native Americans to build his railroad that Ambrose Bierce renamed him Steeland Landford? Should we hold the University of Chicago responsible because its first president, William Rainey Harper, accepted the money to create the university from John D. Rockefeller, who made his fortune by monopolizing the oil industry and by using harsh methods to suppress union supporters seeking to obtain decent wages?

It is even open to question whether it is wrong for a university to accept gifts from donors who are known at the time of the gift to have made their fortunes in unethical ways. Some will argue that a principled university should have nothing to do with money it knows to be so tainted. On the other hand, would the world be a better place if donors who earned their fortune by immoral means were unable to give their money to charitable and other worthwhile causes and were forced to spend their wealth entirely for their own private purposes?

Some commentators may contend that it is unnecessary to debate whether it is immoral for a university to accept gifts of money connected in some fashion to slave labor. Instead, such gifts should arguably be looked on as stolen property that recipients must give back to the rightful owners even if they acquired the property with no knowledge of its provenance. But the report does not merely blame Harvard for accepting gifts from plantation owners who made their fortunes through the use of slaves. It extends culpability to include accepting gifts from shipowners who carried cotton along with other goods from the West Indies to the United States, to warehouse owners who stored the cotton, to mill owners who turned it into cloth, and finally to Harvard and presumably to the many other New England hospitals, schools, symphony orchestras, museums, and the like that benefited from the generosity of donors whose wealth was connected in some way and to some indeterminate extent with raw materials produced by slave labor.

To base the culpability of Harvard on legal decisions that simply order possessors of works of art or other stolen goods to return them to their rightful owners would require a creative extension of legal precedent that requires more justification than the Harvard report provides. A stolen work of art is a tangible object, and its owners or their descendants can usually be ascertained. The stolen art object is obviously the compensation owed, and the rightful owners, or their descendants, will usually be easy to identify. In the case of slavery, however, it will often be very difficult to ascertain who was harmed and to what extent by a ship that carried a portion of the plantation's produce to America, or a mill that turned cotton into cloth.

The report also finds the University morally culpable for employing professors during the nineteenth century, such as Louis Agassiz, who conducted research purporting to demonstrate the intellectual inferiority of the Negro race. This verdict is surely debatable. Agassiz, a world-famous biologist, was appointed by Harvard for his work on fossil fishes, glaciers, and geological epochs rather than race. Should universities be held to have acted immorally for continuing to employ professors such as Agassiz whose views on race were accepted by many people at the time and were only later proven to be incorrect? How can Harvard be considered culpable when firing a professor such as Agassiz would clearly violate the principles of academic freedom? Was Stanford wrong for refusing to fire the Nobel Prize–winning phys-icist William Shockley after he openly proclaimed in the 1960s and 1970s that Blacks were inferior in intelligence to Whites?

AFFIRMATIVE ACTION AS REPARATIONS

Finally, in considering reconciliation and reparations, what weight should be given to a university's efforts since the 1960s to encour-age and subsidize the education of Black students and to support research on the history and accomplishments of Black people? During the past sixty years, Harvard and most other selective universities have made exceptional efforts to recruit Black stu-dents and provide them with enough financial aid to enable them to complete their education. These same institutions have also tried to recruit Black faculty and staff and have funded research on the history of Blacks and their contributions to American life, literature, and culture. Many tens of millions of dollars have been spent every year for these purposes, and more will continue to be spent in the future.

The report describes these initiatives but does not mention them in discussing what Harvard needs to do to atone for its many ties to slavery and racial discrimination. Is there any reason these efforts should not be placed on the scales in considering how a university can come to terms with its past? Some may reply that efforts to assist the education of Blacks and recognize their important place in our history have contributed to the general purposes of the University by adding to the diversity of its student body and the scope of its research. As a result, these measures are arguably part of the normal operation of the institution and hence should not count as a contribution to make up for the many injustices done to Black people in the more distant past.

Having been at Harvard when affirmative action was introduced, I do not consider this argument entirely fair. From the first deliberate attempts to recruit Black students in the early 1960s, the policy has reflected a conviction that making special efforts to educate larger numbers of these students and to foster courses and research on race was the most effective way for Harvard and other universities to help counter the effects of the many laws, practices, and prejudices that had long denied Blacks their right to an equal opportunity to succeed according to their abilities and ambitions. Universities have since come to recognize other important benefits from diversity, but the desire to help overcome the continuing effects of centuries of injustice and exclusion has always been an important motive for all that has been accomplished and all that remains to be done.

In raising all these questions, I do not mean to criticize the writing of the Harvard report. It was admirable to conduct and publish such a detailed and careful account of the many ties that connect the University to slavery and racial discrimination. I agree that it was appropriate to consider Harvard's responsibility for these connections. However, I do not consider it appropriate or fair to deal with the issue of responsibility in such a cursory fashion. By its sweeping assertion of Harvard's moral culpability, the report tacitly assumes that a university is morally responsible for the private lives of its faculty and trustees; that universities should never accept gifts from donors whose fortunes can be linked in any way to slavery or other immoral activities; and that

Harvard is morally at fault if it has continued to employ professors whose theories on matters of race, and other sensitive subjects as well, have been later found to be wrong. By rendering these judgments without discussing the counterarguments and qualifications that could be made, the report fails to give much assistance to other universities grappling with issues of moral responsibility or to throw much light on why a university such as Harvard should feel obliged to offer a substantial sum of money as reparations.

ONE FINAL ARGUMENT FOR REPARATIONS

On further reflection, there is one remaining line of reasoning that may conceivably have led the reparations committee to reach its conclusion that Harvard should offer a substantial sum of reparative money regardless of whether the University was morally responsible for all its previous ties to slavery and to subsequent discriminatory policies that disadvantaged Black people. The committee may have decided that Harvard, along with all White Americans, continues to share in the profits made and the opportunities gained by the cheap labor obtained from slavery and all the subsequent discriminatory practices that have prevented Blacks from enjoying an equal opportunity to live in the best communities, attend the best public schools, and compete for the best jobs. Although many of these discriminatory practices have now been remedied, their effects continue to affect the lives of many Blacks and limit the benefits they might have enjoyed if slavery and widespread discrimination had never existed.

The sense of collective unease on the part of many liberals that they may be reaping benefits derived from decades of slavery and discrimination may make them feel obliged to offer some reparative compensation. It is true that this expansive view of White responsibility has not found favor in the courts and legislatures of the nation. It is also true that the very idea that universities should advantage Blacks to make up for America's history of slavery and discrimination was expressly rejected by Justice Lewis Powell in *Regents of the University of California v. Bakke* as a valid reason for upholding preferential admissions for Blacks.[4] Nevertheless, a lingering concern may remain among many liberal Whites that they are continuing to benefit from a long history of inhumane and discriminatory practices against Blacks.

If this is indeed the basis for Harvard's decision to give a reparative sum of money, the report creates a precedent that could give rise to a host of potential difficulties that neither the committee nor the University saw fit to address. Consider global warming, for example. For fifty years at least, the government of the United States, supported presumably by a majority of voters, failed to take adequate preventive measures, such as carbon taxes and other policies for reducing harmful emissions, despite being aware of the drastic effects of climate change on the environment. During this period, Harvard accepted gifts from donors whose fortunes were derived from fossil fuels. I approved the appointment of a professor who turned out to be a climate-change denier. One member of the six-person senior board of trustees when I first became president was the CEO of a major oil company. Meanwhile, the University continued to emit large quantities of pollutants and only gradually began to make determined efforts to reduce its carbon footprint.

Governments are the obvious source of reparations for the damage done to poor countries as a result of carbon emissions. Nevertheless, if the government does not act, and America and other wealthy countries that have benefited most from continuing to pollute the atmosphere do not make appropriate reparative payments, must Harvard and other elite universities accept a responsibility to pay substantial sums to help compensate Pakistan, Bangladesh, and other low-lying countries that have been hard-hit by global warming?

This is only one of the questions that could arise from the decision to have a university assume an obligation to pay reparations for policies and practices that are later seen to be harmful to others. Because this expansive theory of moral responsibility is clearly not widely acknowledged and could easily give rise to future controversies, it is puzzling why the committee saw fit to announce its conclusion without making clear its reasoning for finding Harvard culpable or explaining why the efforts of the past sixty years to recruit Black students and promote research on Black history and related subjects did not provide atonement enough for its historic ties to slavery and discrimination. As it is, the report's sweeping conclusion regarding Harvard's moral responsibility is not explained, nor does it offer much guidance on how a university should respond in future cases involving its connections with policies or practices that turn out to be misguided and harmful to others.

PART III

———

The Conservative Critique

UNLIKE THE LIBERAL CRITICISMS DISCUSSED IN THE preceding chapters, conservative complaints are typically voiced not by faculty or by students, but by politicians and commentators from outside academia. Many of these accusations are quite hostile. As J. D. Vance, a Yale Law School graduate and senator from Ohio, reportedly declared, "Universities Are the Enemy."[1] According to Donald Trump, "The time has come to reclaim our once great educational institutions from the radical Left, and we will do that."[2]

Two underlying divisions of opinion help account for conservative complaints. In a typical survey from 2019, 59 percent of Republicans held negative opinions of colleges and universities, while only 33 percent felt positive, whereas 67 percent of Democrats had a positive view and only 18 percent expressed the opposite opinion.[3] In another opinion poll from the same year, although a majority of both Democrats and Republicans agreed that higher education was "going in the wrong direction," 79 percent of Republicans cited "professors bringing their political and social views into the classroom" as a major reason, compared with only 17 percent of Democrats.[4]

The second division of opinion reflects the contrast in attitudes of White liberals and White conservatives regarding race and racial discrimination. In a 2019 survey, 72 percent of White liberals believed that "racial discrimination is the main reason why many Black people can't get ahead these days."[5] In contrast, 80 percent of White conservatives agreed with the statement that "Blacks who can't get ahead in this country are mostly responsible for their own condition," and large majorities believed that the real problem is "people seeing discrimination where it really doesn't exist."[6]

Against the backdrop of these sharply divergent views, chapter 6 considers the evidence for the frequent claims by conservative politicians that elite college faculties are indoctrinating students with their liberal views. Chapter 7 discusses the persistent efforts of conservative groups to persuade federal courts to condemn the use of racial preferences by leading universities in admitting minority students to their colleges and professional schools. Finally, chapter 8 describes the efforts by universities to create a more welcoming and supportive environment for all races, genders, and identity groups and examines the conservative charge that these policies are compromising freedom of speech on campus.

CHAPTER 6

———

Are College Students Being
Indoctrinated by Liberal Professors?

A COMMON CONSERVATIVE COMPLAINT ABOUT ELITE universities is that their professors indoctrinate students with their liberal beliefs. The basic argument for this assertion is simple. It is well established that college faculties are predominantly liberal in their social and political opinions. When young people of an impressionable age go to college, often free of parental influence for the first time, their views about society, politics, and government are bound to be affected by the opinions of their professors. As a result, conservatives argue, most college students graduate with decidedly liberal views and make up one of the constituencies that votes most heavily for Democratic candidates.

THE POLITICAL ORIENTATION OF ELITE FACULTIES

There is ample empirical support for the claim that faculties are predominantly liberal. In a careful study published in 2006 that was based on surveys from a wide range of institutions, the authors found that 9.4 percent of faculty members identified as "very liberal," 34.7 percent as "liberal," 18.7 percent as "slightly liberal," 18 percent as "middle of the road," 10.5 percent as "slightly conservative," 8.0 percent as "conservative," and 1.2 percent as "very conservative."[1] By 2016–17, another survey of faculty by the Higher Education Research Institute at UCLA found that 60 percent of professors self-identified as far left or liberal compared to only 12 percent identifying as conservative or far right.[2] In 2023 the *New York Times* reported the same division of liberal and conservative faculty members as the HERI report five years before.[3] These figures may understate the risk of indoctrination, since it is well established that conservative professors are more likely to teach courses on science or engineering that seldom raise political issues rather than subjects such as political science and sociology, where faculty members are especially likely to be liberals.

I am unaware of any survey that records the political orientation of faculty from elite colleges as a whole. In 2022, however, the *Harvard Crimson,* a student newspaper, conducted a survey of Harvard's Arts and Sciences faculty and discovered the startling fact that only 1.6 percent of the several hundred respondents described themselves as conservatives.[4] I know of no evidence to suggest that this condition differs greatly from that of most other elite universities.

A casual observer learning of these results might well assume that liberal professors must be discriminating against conservative candidates in choosing appointees to the faculty. The evidence on faculty hiring, however, casts doubt on this conclusion. The most authoritative study on the question compared the careers of conservative and liberal professors teaching similar subjects.[5] The authors found only a slight tendency toward liberal favoritism and acknowledged that even this small difference might be caused by some overlooked variable having nothing to do with liberal bias.

ARE STUDENTS BEING INDOCTRINATED?

The fact that liberal professors greatly outnumber conservatives does not prove that liberals indoctrinate their students. On this vital point, the evidence is quite equivocal. Conservatives often cite a survey of college seniors in which 49 percent replied that liberal professors discussed their political views "frequently" or "all the time" while only 9 percent said the same thing about conservative professors.[6] Apparently, instructors revealed their political views whether or not they were germane to the course.

Since large majorities of the faculty are liberal, one could easily infer from this survey that indoctrination must be occurring. The survey by itself, however, does not prove that the political views expressed by instructors have any effect on their students. In fact, another survey of more than 7,000 students from more than 120 colleges found that although 48 percent of the respondents had come to view liberals more favorably since entering college, 50 percent viewed conservatives more favorably.[7] Similarly, while 31 percent of respondents viewed conservatives *less* favorably, 30 percent became less favorable toward liberals.[8] In still another survey reported in the *Washington Post*, when students were asked whether they felt pressured in class to change their political orientation, an "overwhelming majority" replied that they did not.[9]

There is convincing evidence, however, that conservative students feel intimidated in class about expressing their views on controversial issues. According to a survey by a higher education team from Intelligent.com in September 2021, 55 percent of conservative students acknowledged being afraid to voice their political opinions.[10] Nevertheless, the same survey went on to point out that 49 percent of liberals were likewise reluctant to speak.[11] Moreover, several surveys have found that the reason most students feel inhibited from expressing their opinions is their concern over the reaction of their fellow students, not the behavior of their instructors.[12] For example, in a Knight Foundation survey of undergraduates in 2019, 68 percent acknowledged that they refrained from expressing their political views in class but attributed their reluctance to a fear that their classmates would find them offensive.[13]

Finally, a study conducted in 2020 by a team of researchers for Ohio State traced the evolution of student views toward conservatives and liberals in a large sample of colleges through their four years of study. The survey found that student opinion about liberals gradually became more positive throughout the four years, but that student views about conservatives also rose appreciably, from 42 to 50 percent during the freshman and sophomore years before reverting to 42 percent by their senior year.[14]

As the authors pointed out, moreover, the decline in positive impressions about conservatives during the last two years may well have resulted from students' concerns about the policies of Donald Trump and not from their interaction with faculty or classmates. The denial of global warming by Trump and many Republicans as well as their opposition to abortion could well have upset many college students. That argument gains support from the fact that recent college graduates gave approximately half their votes in 2004 to George W. Bush (as they did for Ronald Reagan as well) and only shifted heavily to Democrats when Trump became president.

All in all, therefore, it is difficult to conclude from the evidence whether liberal professors are indoctrinating their students. The students themselves tend not to think so. The changes that occur in their political opinions during college are not large, nor do they show a clear tendency toward increased liberalism. Where liberal sentiments do increase, there is no convincing evidence to prove whether the change is caused by professors, by other students, by politicians, or by events in the world beyond college.

Incidentally, there is also little evidence that conservative students have more negative views of college than their liberal classmates or that they are treated less well by the faculty. In fact, investigators in one survey found that conservatives enjoy college more, have closer relations with the faculty, and receive slightly higher grades than their liberal classmates.[15]

ARE FACULTIES TOO LIBERAL?

Do these findings mean that elite universities have no reason to be worried about the predominantly liberal beliefs of their professors? By no means. On the contrary, there are at least three reasons for concern.

First of all, discussions among members of departments in the social sciences and in some other fields as well are likely to lose something valuable if all the participants share a similar liberal orientation. The quality of conversations about politics, economics, or society in general is bound to benefit if the participants hold different beliefs about what considerations need to be taken into account and how much weight to accord to each of the various factors and values that bear on a final judgment. Liberal professors may insist that they are quite familiar with conservative thought, but familiarity is unlikely to be an adequate substitute for actually having colleagues with a different opinion actively participating in the conversation.

A second problem with the current ideological makeup of most faculties involves its effect on students. It is now obvious to all that the nation is suffering from the deep divide between liberals and conservatives that has crippled the political process, diminished the confidence of the public in established institutions, and caused many people to avoid speaking to one another about a growing list of contentious subjects. People from both sides of the political divide increasingly live in two separate bubbles in which they receive their news about the world from different sources that reinforce the contrasting views of each rival faction about what is happening in the world and who is responsible for all that has gone wrong. In view of these conditions, every university ought to be considering what it can do to help both factions engage in civil discussion with each other. Such an effort is bound to be more difficult to arrange, however, if almost all faculty members share a fundamentally liberal outlook. To their credit, a number of universities are trying to address this problem by arranging discussions within classes or outside them in which liberal and conservative students are encouraged to argue with one another about controversial issues. Many colleges and universities, however, are not even doing that.

The third disadvantage from the near absence of conservative faculty is the risk that Republican politicians will intervene to try to compensate for the political imbalance among university professors. Governor Ron DeSantis of Florida (a graduate of Yale College and Harvard Law School) has led the way in this endeavor. He has signed legislation into law that calls for regular surveys of faculty to ascertain their political orientation and seeks to have trustees play a more active role in faculty appointments. He has sought to dictate how college instructors teach the history and current state of race relations and has even supported a law that allows students to bring video cameras into the classroom, presumably to record instances of indoctrination by professors. His most recent undertaking is to transform a highly regarded state college into an avowedly conservative institution.

Interventions of this kind are not confined to Florida. In North Carolina, the politically appointed regents of the flagship university actually revoked the offer of an appointment to the faculty of a prominent Black journalist because of her writing about the history of Black people in America. In other predominantly Republican states, legislators have defunded courses that teach material that is thought to involve critical race theory.

These intrusions by politicians into college teaching should sound the alarm in every university. Not surprisingly, such interventions are much more likely to occur when faculties become predominantly one-sided in their political views.

APPOINTING MORE CONSERVATIVE INSTRUCTORS

What is it, then, that elite universities can do to improve on the current situation? There is no easy answer. Conservative professors capable of being appointed to the faculty of elite universities are often hard to find. College teaching appears to be a profession that consistently attracts more liberals than conservatives. Clearly, one cannot and should not expect universities to lower their intellectual standards for choosing professors simply to hire more conservatives. But there are other steps that universities could take.

The only elite faculty I know that has deliberately grappled with this problem is the Kennedy School of Government at Harvard. The faculty understood the need for a school of public policy to provide a variety of political views. It also recognized the practical difficulty of achieving an adequate balance of political opinion by simply trying to find suitable appointments to the tenured faculty. As a result, it addressed the problem in other ways as well—by hiring "instructors from practice" on multiyear appointments, such as Mickey Edwards, the former third-ranking Republican in the House of Representatives, who taught courses on American politics; a retired Republican senator, Alan Simpson, who spent several years as head of the Institute of Politics; David Gergen, who worked on the White House staff as an adviser to more than one Republican president and served as co-chair of the Kennedy School's Program on Leadership; and most recently, Arthur C. Brooks, former head of the conservative American Enterprise Institute. Most of these individuals and others like them were effective teachers and excellent colleagues who were welcomed by the rest of the faculty.

There are a variety of other ways by which faculties can address the dearth of conservative colleagues. They can try to bring such professors as visitors for a semester or a year. In order not to overlook promising candidates for the faculty, they can require departments to demonstrate specific efforts to find conservative scholars who might be suitable candidates for tenure or a tenure-track appointment. They can encourage social science departments to make special efforts to encourage promising conservative students to apply to their PhD programs and thus become possible future candidates for a faculty appointment at their own or some other university.

Different universities will undoubtedly find varying ways to address the underlying problem. Whatever the solution, the faculty must be an essential participant in finding a solution. Thus, the immediate step for academic leaders to consider is to help professors recognize that a problem exists and then to launch an effort with the faculty to formulate specific plans to try to improve on the existing situation.

The challenge of creating more political diversity in elite college faculties is not at all easy, and progress will undoubtedly be slow if appropriate academic standards are maintained. Yet the task seems no more difficult than the challenge of appointing more women and minority professors during the last few decades of the twentieth century. Fortunately, most members of existing faculties appear to agree that the lack of political diversity is a legitimate problem.[16] Once they realize that they will not be pressured to compromise their normal intellectual standards for tenure, they should be willing to work with the administration to try to solve the problem.

CHAPTER 7

The Campaign against Racial
Preferences as Elite Universities Seek
to Diversify Their Student Bodies

M Y DECADES-LONG INVOLVEMENT WITH ISSUES OF race at Harvard began just after I received tenure at the Law School. In 1962, at a meeting of the faculty, Dean Erwin Griswold, a staunch Republican with a distinctly autocratic style of leadership, made a surprising announcement. The issue of race, he declared, was the most important problem facing America, and the outcome was in large part being decided in the courts. "And yet," he continued, "I see virtually no black faces among our students nor among the student bodies of other leading law schools. That," he added firmly, "has to change."

When Griswold spoke, I suspect that there were few Black college students in America who even imagined coming to Harvard Law School. Barely 1 percent of the nation's lawyers were African American. If Black undergraduates even knew about Harvard Law, they probably regarded it as a distant place for well-to-do White students that would probably not admit them and would certainly cost far more than they could afford.

The dean, however, and his able vice dean Louis Toepfer had a plan. Harvard would create a summer program for juniors at Historically Black Colleges and Universities. These students would come to Cambridge for a few weeks, with all expenses paid, to get a taste of law school classes, listen to a few Black judges and lawyers describe what careers in law were like, and—most important—discover that Harvard Law School was genuinely interested in having Blacks apply. Once they were admitted, Harvard would provide them with enough financial aid to make their legal education affordable.

The hope was that students in the program would return to their colleges for their senior year and spread the word about Harvard Law School so that some of their classmates would apply. Very few Black students responded the first year. Since I was a member of the admissions committee at the time, I remember how much weaker their academic records were in comparison with the test scores and college grades of most of the White students we admitted. Yet we accepted almost all of them, and I believe they all managed to graduate, even though they may have had to struggle to finish. As we repeated the program each summer, however, the number and the quality of Black applicants grew steadily. Naive as we all were at the time, we thought we had solved the problem that the dean had presented to us.

During the summer program in 1968, however, as racial protests continued to roil the nation, the mood of the Black students abruptly changed. They seemed angrier, less deferential, and more inclined to ask difficult questions about the absence of Black faculty members and the lack of any courses on race and the law. Although we didn't know it then, we were about to encounter a whole series of problems on the way to becoming a truly diverse institution.

We had clearly not anticipated all the consequences of bringing a substantial number of Black students to the Law School. We were slow to realize that these new arrivals would expect some recognition in the curriculum of the long, troubled influence of race in the legal policies, institutions, and administrative practices of this country. We did not fully recognize the importance to students of having Black scholars on our faculty and Black administrators on our staff who understood the special challenges and strains that minorities encountered on entering an institution unused to their presence. It was only when Blacks enrolled in substantial numbers and began to make demands that the Law School responded.

It would have been asking a lot of law schools to expect them to anticipate all these issues. The problem of assimilating minority students and making them feel at home was terra incognita for Harvard and other prominent law schools. While we could and did attempt to hire Black colleagues who could help us appreciate the difficulties and devise solutions, it was by no means easy to find qualified Black faculty and administrators for a law school in the 1960s when only 1 percent of the nation's lawyers were African American.

Our progress in dealing with these problems was slow but continuous. By the end of my presidency, I felt pleased with all that Harvard had done. The number and quality of Black students throughout the University had increased substantially, and the student body was thoroughly integrated. Even the singing group for Black spirituals included several White members. Although the number of Black professors was still quite modest, the quality of these scholars was impressive. Research in African American studies was about to flourish under the leadership of Henry Louis Gates Jr.

Many years after I had retired, I was reminded of the long struggle to diversify the student body at Harvard. The occasion for this response was a reunion dinner of Black Law School alumni. I had been invited along with Walter Leonard, my longtime comrade-in-arms at the Law School and the president's office, to receive the Black alumni's Freedom Medal for our efforts to promote the education of Black law students in the late 1960s and early 1970s. The banquet took place in a huge tent on the lawn in front of the Law School and was attended by several hundred alumni. Our most famous graduate was unable to attend, being occupied with more urgent matters in the White House. As I mingled with the audience, however, I noticed more than one CEO of a large corporation, a goodly number of judges, professors, public officials, and scores of partners in law firms. The evening was full of laughter and good spirits. As I left the tent to return home, I could not help feeling that looking back over the years, the long and still unfinished effort to diversify the student body, with all of its difficulties and anxious moments, was one of the most satisfying and worthwhile experiences of my entire professional career.

THE FIGHT FOR RACIAL PREFERENCE IN ADMISSIONS

Not everyone in America approved of the effort to increase the number of Black students. As enrollments of these students in elite universities continued to grow, opponents began to contest the use of preferential admissions for minority students by bringing suit in the federal courts. In the mid-1970s, a white student, Allan Bakke, had applied to medical school at the University of California at Davis and was denied. Because he knew that minority students with less impressive academic records than his had been admitted, he brought suit claiming a violation of his right to equal treatment.

When Bakke's case was accepted for review by the Supreme Court, our general counsel, Daniel Steiner, flew to California and, by some miracle of persuasion, obtained an agreement from the state university to let my former colleague at the Law School, Archibald Cox, argue the case before the Supreme Court. Archie had previously served as solicitor general of the United States and had appeared in many cases before the Court, winning an enviable reputation among the justices for his ability and integrity. He quickly assembled a team of leading professors of constitutional law to prepare a brief and subsequently argued the case before the Court in Washington.

The justices eventually issued a decision by a divided Court.[1] In the decisive opinion, Justice Lewis Powell declared that racial quotas were unlawful and that racial preferences to atone for slavery or other forms of racial discrimination were also illegal. But racial preferences to obtain the educational benefits of a diverse student body would be permitted provided that race was treated as merely one factor among others in gaining admission. In a rare tribute to Harvard, the lead opinion included as an appendix the official description of our procedure for admitting students to the college as an example of what the Court regarded as the proper way to use race.

The conservative opponents of race-sensitive admissions did not accept the *Bakke* case as final but continued to attack the use of race either by introducing ballot initiatives in various states or by bringing suit in federal courts. In the 1990s two cases challenging the admissions policies of the University of Michigan seemed destined once again to reach the Supreme Court.

At this point, five years after I had retired as president, Martin Michaelson, a former deputy general counsel at Harvard and now a prominent Washington lawyer representing universities, came to my office and asked me to write an op-ed essay defending the use of race in admissions. I immediately refused. "There have already been plenty of essays on this subject," I said. "What is needed now is not another restatement of the arguments but some reliable facts about how the use of race has actually worked in practice."

As I spoke, the ideal solution suddenly occurred to me. I knew that my former counterpart at Princeton, William Bowen, then the president of the Andrew W. Mellon Foundation, had compiled a massive database containing the results of extensive surveys of former students from twenty-eight highly selective colleges and universities. This sample included a few large, elite public institutions, such as the universities of Michigan and North Carolina, some highly selective private universities, including Yale and Princeton, and several small private liberal arts colleges, such as Wesleyan and Bryn Mawr. "With this data," I said, "Bill might be able to discover a lot about the effects of using race in admissions."

Michaelson subsequently approached Bowen and asked whether he would conduct such a study. Bill declined, saying that his database had been compiled for an entirely different purpose. A few days later, however, he called me and said that he had had second thoughts about the proposal. He would undertake the study if I joined him as a co-author. I agreed and the project immediately got under way.

We realized at the outset that the data might turn out to show that race-sensitive admissions had not worked well. Such a finding would be an embarrassment for a great many colleges. Even so, we concluded, it would be far better to discover the results and make them known than to continue with a program that wasn't working.

As it happened, the results we published in a book entitled *The Shape of the River* turned out to be very supportive.[2] Critics of affirmative action had frequently argued that admitting minority students with academic qualifications below those of Whites would ultimately hurt the very students it was meant to help by forcing Blacks to compete with more qualified White students. Our study showed that the opposite was true. Graduation rates for Black and Latino students from the highly selective colleges in Bowen's database were much higher than those of minority students of similar ability who had attended less selective colleges. In fact, the more selective the college, the higher the graduation rates of Black and Latino students turned out to be.[3]

The same was true for the earnings of Black and Latino students after they had graduated from college. Moreover, far from suffering from competing with White students possessing more impressive academic credentials, 90 percent of Black alumni from the selective colleges declared that they were either "very satisfied" (over 60 percent) or "somewhat satisfied" (approximately 30 percent) with their college experience.[4] These figures were almost identical to the results for Whites. Finally, large majorities of both White and minority graduates believed that their college should either maintain or increase its efforts to enroll minority students.[5]

Supportive as our study of affirmative action turned out to be, not all of its findings were positive. We discovered that Black students from selective colleges received lower grades than their White classmates. In fact, their grades were significantly *below* what one would have expected on the basis of their SAT scores and high school records.[6] This tendency has persisted not only for Black students but, to a lesser extent, for Latino students as well.[7]

Researchers have struggled to find the reason for this consistent underperformance in the classroom. The most convincing explanation is that of "stereotype threat" developed through a series of experiments by the psychologist Claude Steele.[8] This theory holds that minority students (along with women in mathematics classes) are aware of a stereotype in many people's minds that minorities (and women in math) are less capable than White men. When minority students (or women in math) encounter a test that they believe might confirm their inferiority, they do poorly, but if they can be persuaded that the test is not designed for this purpose, they do as well as their White male classmates.

Subsequent inquiries seem to bear out this theory but tend to find that it does not provide a complete explanation for the underperformance of minorities. Other studies have found that courses on race relations, along with added measures to make minority students feel welcome, seem to help. Appointing larger numbers of minority instructors and support staff may also do some good. All in all, however, underperformance remains a condition that as yet has been neither fully explained nor fully remedied.

Several years after our book appeared, the two cases against the University of Michigan reached the Supreme Court. Once again, the fate of race-sensitive admissions hung in the balance. And once again, the Court upheld the practice by a narrow margin, provided that race was only one of several factors entering into the admission of minority students.[9] A strong majority opinion written by Justice Sandra Day O'Connor cited our book, along with another study that the Mellon Foundation had sponsored, to support its finding that diverse classes had an important educational value for White students as well as Blacks.

In her opinion, Justice O'Connor accurately described the two principal reasons we had identified that justified the use of racial preferences—not only because of the educational value of diversity but also because of the need in a democracy to avoid having a predominantly White leadership class presiding over an increasingly diverse population in important occupations such as politics, government service, business, and the military. This point had been strongly affirmed by statements to the Court supporting race-conscious admissions signed by large numbers of CEOs of major companies and by former superintendents of the three military academies.

Since the publication of our book in 1998, many studies have been published confirming the educational value of a diverse student body. Researchers have found that the interaction of White and minority students in classes and extracurricular activities yields a surprisingly broad array of educational benefits. The latest volume in a series summarizing hundreds of studies of all kinds on the effects of undergraduate education found a consensus that diversity leads to student gains in a wide variety of respects, including writing ability, racial identity development, drive to achieve, intellectual self-confidence, well-being, personal and social development, civic attitudes and behaviors, positive diversity attitudes, gender-role progressiveness, and LGBTQ attitudes.[10] Overall, the study concluded, "in the review for this volume, the most impressive and consistent findings for any form of interpersonal involvement occur from interpersonal diversity interactions."[11]

These results take on added importance in view of the widespread residential segregation that still exists throughout the United States. Because of this practice, large percentages of young people in America grow up in communities and go to schools that are predominantly minority or White. For these students, enrolling in college can afford them their first experience of living, going to class, and socializing with classmates of a different race. With their many courses, student housing, and extracurricular activities that bring different students together, highly selective colleges provide an ideal environment to prepare young people to live in an increasingly diverse society. The protests that raged across the country in the aftermath of George Floyd's killing gave powerful evidence of the continuing need for greater understanding among the races even as the numbers of young Whites among the marching crowds suggested the progress already made.

EVALUATING THE RECORD

All in all, despite the problems that remain, elite colleges such as Harvard have good reason to be pleased with what they have achieved in assembling and graduating a more racially diverse student body. As Professor Melvin Urofsky concludes at the end of his detailed history of race-sensitive admissions, "Affirmative action has worked in that hundreds of thousands of people who would have been barred from colleges or from the workplace have gotten in, have gotten an education or a job."[12] In 1960, before universities began using racial preferences, Blacks made up only 1.2 percent of the nation's lawyers, 2.8 percent of doctors, and 0.5 percent of engineers, and virtually none were CEOs of large corporations. In government, only four members of Congress (and no senators) were Black, along with only four federal judges, three mayors, no cabinet members, and very few military commanders. Today, more than 5 percent of lawyers, doctors, and engineers are Black. Less progress has been made in business, but a record eight Blacks are now presidents of

Fortune 500 companies. In government, some sixty cities with populations over 40,000 now have Black mayors. More than fifty members of the House of Representatives are Black, along with three members of the Senate and 11 percent of all federal judges. In the armed services, some 58 (5.6 percent) of generals and admirals are Black. As a result, Blacks have gained a strong voice in the government offices, judges' chambers, leading law firms, executive suites, and other venues where social policies are made.

Although preferential admissions are not the only cause of this progress, they have undoubtedly played a part. Their importance is clearly reflected in the strong support for racial preferences expressed by the superintendents of the armed service academies, the CEOs of major corporations, the American Bar Association, and the American Medical Association in statements submitted to the Supreme Court during cases involving affirmative action.

THE BATTLE OVER RACIAL
PREFERENCES CONTINUES

Despite the *Grutter* case, conservative organizations persisted in their attack in federal courts over the use of racial preferences by highly selective universities. Although the Supreme Court narrowed the use of preferences in minor ways, a bare majority of the justices continued to uphold the practice. Eventually, however, in 2014, Edward Blum, director of the Students for Fair Admissions, again brought suit, this time against Harvard and the University of North Carolina. In these cases, he advanced the novel argument that both these universities discriminated against highly qualified Asian applicants in order to make room for Black students admitted by racial preference. The federal district judge upheld Harvard's use of race, as did the Court of Appeals. Undaunted, Blum appealed to the Supreme Court, and a majority of the justices agreed to hear the case.

In arguing the case, Harvard faced a much more conservative court than the one that decided *Grutter* or *Bakke*. As most observers had expected, a majority of justices voted to condemn Harvard's admissions practices. The end of minority preferences had long been predicted. The use of race in deciding who should be admitted to selective colleges never found much favor among the public as a whole, even among liberals. Some opinion polls found that as many as 70 percent of the respondents opposed the practice. Even Justice O'Connor, in writing the lead opinion in *Grutter,* expressed the hope that racial preferences would no longer be needed in another twenty-five years.

Now that the Supreme Court has spoken, what are the likely effects of its decision on the diversity of student bodies in elite universities? Although the demise of preferential admissions will almost certainly reduce the number of Blacks and Latinos, significant numbers will still be admitted. Some will have good enough high school grades and test scores to be accepted without any preference. Others will be athletes, or will receive a boost because they come from low-income families.* Still others may enroll as selective universities such as Harvard and

---

*Richard Kahlenberg has long argued that selective colleges could be just as diverse without affirmative action if they substituted income-based admissions in place of racial preferences. See Kahlenberg, *The Remedy: Class, Race, and Affirmative Action* (1997). Most careful studies, however, disagree with this statement. See, for example, Sean Reardon et al., *Can Socioeconomic Status Substitute for Race in Affirmative Action College Admissions Policies? Evidence from a Simulation Model* (2015); Anthony P. Carnevale, Zachary Mabel, and Kathryn Peltier Campbell, *Race-Conscious Affirmative Action: What's Next* (2023).

North Carolina become more adept at locating academically qualified minority students and persuading them to apply for admission.

In presenting its case to the Supreme Court, Harvard predicted that the number of minority students in its entering classes would drop by more than 50 percent if racial preferences were declared unlawful. In evaluating this estimate, it may be useful to examine the experience in states such as California and Michigan, where racial preferences have long been prohibited by state law. In each case, the percentage admitted to the state's flagship university dropped by 50 percent or more after racial preferences were outlawed. Over the years, however, as the institutions involved began to make greater efforts to recruit minority students with the necessary credentials, the percentages of Black and Latino students gradually increased to cut the initial decline by almost half.

While the experience of the Universities of Michigan and California is suggestive, it is important to note that the conditions for evaluating the admission of minority students are no longer what they were when racial preferences in these states were prohibited. For many years, the most important factors in deciding whom to admit were the applicant's high school grade-point average (GPA) and SAT or ACT scores. Over time, however, the GPA has become less and less accurate for assessing the ability of candidates since grading and grade inflation vary significantly from one high school to another. The SAT and ACT tests have also become less reliable tools for comparing candidates as their predictive value has proved to be weaker than previously thought and the increased use of tutoring has further undermined their usefulness. Because of these problems, most colleges have made submission of test scores optional, diminishing their usefulness even more.

The Supreme Court's majority opinion has further complicated the process of comparing the way admissions officers treat different groups of applicants. Although a majority of the court prohibited the award of preferences to entire groups, it explicitly upheld the right of colleges and universities to consider "how race affected [an individual applicant's] life, be it through discrimination, inspiration or otherwise."

This formulation may seem fair and sensible on its face, but it opens a Pandora's box of problems for anyone seeking to evaluate and compare the accounts from a multitude of minorities and other applicants concerning the personal hardships they have encountered. How can admissions officers determine whether such statements are accurate? How can a court decide whether admissions officers have given equal weight to the problems overcome by minority applicants and the variety of different obstacles surmounted by applicants of other races? It will be virtually impossible for judges to evaluate a university's use of race by reading and comparing hundreds of essays from applicants describing the many different hardships they have encountered. Instead, judges will probably resort to rules of thumb and other simplifying assumptions to determine whether a university has correctly applied the Supreme Court's decision. How reasonable will these assumptions be, and how accurately will they reflect the actual difficulties experienced by the applicants?

As I ponder these uncertainties, I feel more and more uncomfortable. While racial preferences were not ideal, they did a lot of good not only by increasing opportunities for minorities but by enhancing the quality of education for all students. As Bill Bowen and I discovered in our study of racial preferences in twenty-eight selective colleges, undergraduates of all races favored the continuation or expansion of affirmative action programs.[13] Nevertheless, a majority of the Supreme Court dismissed these benefits without a word of recognition. I regret their decision. Although much has been accomplished over the past sixty years, significant obstacles still hamper the progress of minorities, including the continued existence of highly segregated schools and neighborhoods, continued discrimination in finding jobs and obtaining credit, and large and stubborn differences in wealth and average income.

At this point, it is impossible to predict what the future holds. Conceivably, something as beneficial as affirmative action will emerge from the current confusion. Whatever happens, however, one thing does seem clear. Most elite colleges and universities will maintain their commitment to racial diversity. They will do what they can within the limits of the law to make the most of the remaining possibilities for admitting a diverse student body and creating greater opportunities for minorities. I wish them every success in this worthy endeavor.

CHAPTER 8

———

Have Elite Universities Sacrificed Freedom of Speech in Their Effort to Provide a Supportive Environment for All Students?

S STUDENT BODIES ACROSS THE NATION GREW MORE diverse in the 1970s and 1980s, universities began to experience incidents of hostile or intolerant behavior not only toward Blacks but also against women, gays, Asians, and other groups of undergraduates. Bigoted individuals would attach a Nazi swastika to a Jewish student's door; fraternity members would wear blackface at one of their parties; or male students would find ways to insult their gay classmates. At Harvard, a senior hung a Confederate flag out the window of her residence hall, provoking a protest by Black students and a demand that I immediately order the flag to be taken down.*

In response to such incidents, identity groups of students became increasingly sensitive to these provocations, emboldened

---

*I refused to do so on First Amendment grounds and issued a statement to students and faculty explaining the reasons for my decision. Little did I know that one of the Black student leaders discussing what to do about the flag would one day take her place as a justice of the U.S. Supreme Court.

by a growing determination on the part of Blacks and other minorities to fight back. Most of their protests were in response to obviously prejudiced or hostile behavior. Not infrequently, however, their complaints involved behavior of a kind that many people would have previously considered innocuous.

Meanwhile, various research studies had appeared asserting that the discomfort felt by students who felt unwelcome and disrespected could lead to poorer academic performance or even dropping out of college.[1] Microaggressions against minorities were also found to contribute to the "stereotype threats" described by the psychologist Claude Steele, which created a tendency on the part of minority students to perform academically below the level predicted by their SAT scores and high school grades.[2]

In response to these developments, campus leaders grew increasingly convinced of the need to do more to discourage hostile or disrespectful behavior and provide a more supportive environment for their increasingly diverse student bodies. Many colleges sought to protect minorities, women, and LGBTQ students from verbal abuse by enacting detailed speech codes that defined various kinds of prohibited communication. Some of these codes were very restrictive, prohibiting even such vague behaviors as "leering, ogling, derogatory jokes, and inappropriately directed laughter."

Meanwhile, efforts to silence speakers who uttered insensitive or disrespectful remarks provoked complaints from commentators and even from prominent figures such as President George H. W. Bush, who condemned the plague of "political correctness" that inhibited free discussion on many campuses. Civil libertarians such as Alan Kors and Harvey Silverglate launched an uncompromising attack on almost any attempt to limit speech on campus.[3] When challenged by those who felt there should be *some* prohibited speech that is too hateful and hurtful to be tolerated, they argued that once universities ventured down this path, they were likely to find themselves on a slippery slope that would ultimately lead to ridiculously broad and detailed speech codes of the kind that had already been adopted on numerous campuses. Many universities, however, rejected the civil libertarian view as too insensitive to the compelling need to provide a welcoming environment for all students so that they could adjust to the academic demands of college without feeling unwanted or looked down on as inferior by their classmates.

THE RESPONSE OF THE COURTS

By now, the federal courts have offered some help to address this difference of opinion and to clarify the application of the U.S. Constitution to colleges and universities. It is clear, first of all, that the First Amendment gives the right of free speech to professors and to students, at least in public (or state) universities. As a result, almost every federal court that has considered campus speech codes has condemned them as overly broad.

At the same time, however, the Supreme Court has also upheld the application of a federal law against sexual harassment to cases of verbal abuse of female employees by male supervisors or employers.[4] The Court has subsequently applied this ruling to include the harassment of female students in colleges and universities.[5] In doing so, however, the justices limited the definition of illegal harassment to speech that is directed at an individual and is "severe, pervasive, and objectively offensive and that so undermines and detracts from the victims' educational experience that the victims are effectively denied equal access to an institution's resources and opportunities."

The definition of harassment provided by the Court would appear to allow campus authorities to prohibit persistent efforts to denigrate one or a group of students and drive them out of the university. If so, students who repeatedly posted signs demanding that "Blacks go home" would presumably be subject to discipline. Lower court decisions, however, have made clear that judges will not allow universities to penalize students or others for disrespectful or even hateful remarks expressed in a single conversation or document. Campus codes of conduct prohibiting "leering, ogling, derogatory jokes, and inappropriately directed laughter" will continue to be found unconstitutional, at least in public or state universities.

Even in a state university, freedom of speech does not allow students to disrupt classes or otherwise interfere with the orderly teaching of professors. Nor does the First Amendment protect students who disrupt speeches by controversial figures, or who harass other students to a degree sufficient to interfere with their education. Even so, there is no clear line as yet to distinguish unacceptable behavior from protected speech.

Similar difficulties complicate judicial attempts to define the limits of freedom of speech for university professors. For example, in *Garcetti v. Ceballos,* the Court upheld the right of a mayor to fire a city official who publicly criticized the administration that employed him, notwithstanding the First Amendment.[6] In the lead opinion, however, the justices indicated that different considerations might apply in cases involving professors who criticized their universities. The opinion did not elaborate but left the issue to be resolved in a future case. It is possible therefore that the *Garcetti* case could be construed as giving states the power to dictate how professors in their public universities can and cannot teach about controversial subjects such as race relations.*

*The Republican governor and legislature in Florida have recently claimed that what professors in public universities teach and how they teach it are subject to regulation by the State, citing the *Garcetti* case. Accordingly, the Florida state legislature, acting on the initiative of the Republican governor, has prohibited any training or instruction that promotes any of eight enumerated concepts regarding race and gender. This legislation has been challenged in a lawsuit brought by university professors. Sarah Brown and Francie Diep, "Speaking for the State," *Chronicle of Higher Education,* October 14, 2022, p. 10.

The amount of discretion enjoyed by professors in the classroom is also uncertain. Instructors have traditionally had considerable freedom to teach as they choose under the First Amendment and the doctrine of academic freedom. Nevertheless, neither academic freedom, as defined by the Association of American University Professors (AAUP), nor the First Amendment will protect attempts by instructors to indoctrinate their students, while academic freedom protects only the expression of ideas that are germane to the subjects of the course. The First Amendment protects a wider range of speech but presumably does not interfere with efforts by university administrators to discourage instructors from insulting students or wasting inordinate amounts of time in class discussing matters unrelated to the subject of the course.

Neither the First Amendment nor the doctrine of academic freedom, however, is very clear on what kinds of administrative action constitute an unwarranted violation of a professor's freedom. Firing instructors for their views is clearly forbidden. But what if the administration does not fire instructors or dock their pay but either asks them to stop teaching a particular course or creates an alternative section of the course with another instructor to accommodate students who feel that their professor is insensitive or possibly prejudiced against them in grading their exams?

THE CURRENT CONFUSION

Amid the many uncertainties about the extent of protection accorded to free speech, a number of cases have come to light in which university administrations have imposed questionable limitations on the freedom of students and faculty members to express themselves. On one occasion, for example, students returning on a bus from an athletic contest were disciplined for singing a racist song. Fraternities have suffered penalties for holding costume parties in which members wore blackface. At one public university, two professors were forced to resign after evidence came to light that one of them had appeared seven years before at a student party dressed in a Confederate uniform while the second came wearing blackface. At another prominent public university, a faculty member had his appointment revoked for having made intemperate remarks on Twitter about the prime minister of Israel and his government's treatment of Palestinians in the West Bank.

In the aftermath of the brutal killing of George Floyd and a spate of other fatal shootings of Black men and women by city police, many colleges have redoubled their efforts to discourage the expression of disrespectful or controversial views on campus. In their zeal, officials have sometimes acted in ways that seem at odds with the principle of free expression of ideas. For example, several colleges have abruptly canceled speeches on campus by prominent conservatives who have publicly supported policies strongly opposed by minority groups and sympathetic White students. In one widely publicized instance in 2021, MIT even blocked a speech by a prominent scientist on the subject of climate change because he had published an article some years before opposing the use of race in evaluating candidates for academic positions or admission to a university.[7]

A number of cases have also been reported over the past few years in which professors have been asked to withdraw from teaching courses for using words or images that members of the class considered insensitive or disrespectful. In one elite state university, for example, a professor in the School of Music, Theater and Dance was asked to stop teaching an undergraduate class on film in the wake of intense student pressure for having shown a motion picture version of *Othello* starring Laurence

Olivier wearing blackface in the title role. The professor issued an abject apology, but that was not deemed enough, and he stopped teaching the class, although he kept his job and his salary.

Similar treatment has been given to instructors even for statements made years earlier. At one Ivy League institution, an assistant professor of government teaching a course on a subject having nothing to do with race was discovered to have written an article as an undergraduate objecting to the use of racial preferences in admitting students. Although his opinion is shared by a majority of Americans, the dean arranged another section of his course for students who were too upset by his statement to feel comfortable in his class.

Another questionable practice common to many colleges and elite professional schools is asking students seeking admission and individuals applying for academic positions to list previous work they have done to further diversity, equality, and inclusion and to describe any plans they have to make similar efforts in the future. These questions are reminiscent of the ill-fated loyalty oaths in the 1950s at the University of California. They put great pressure on applicants to profess a particular set of beliefs and thus seem clearly at odds with the spirit of academic freedom and the First Amendment.

Examples such as these suggest that many colleges and universities are responding to the problem of reconciling First Amendment principles with an understandable desire to make their students feel welcome and respected by simply endorsing both objectives without explaining how they fit together. These colleges tend to react to student demands by banning controversial speakers from giving lectures on their campus or by removing professors from teaching courses for expressing opinions now or in the past opposing racial preferences or uttering words or opinions that seem disrespectful to many students. At the same time, they continue to proclaim in their official literature their firm commitment to academic freedom and the free exchange of ideas.

The ambivalence of these university officials is matched by a similar confusion among students and faculty. Both groups express strong agreement in principle with the importance of free speech. Yet one-quarter of all faculty members also believe that universities should discipline professors who express hostile views toward women, minorities, or other groups. Students are similarly ambivalent. A large majority claimed to support free speech in a survey of undergraduates conducted by the Brookings Institution in 2017.[8] Yet a majority in the same survey also agreed that it is important for colleges to create a positive learning environment for all students by prohibiting speech or the expression of viewpoints that are offensive or biased against certain groups of people.

The current policy on many campuses of claiming to uphold the First Amendment while intervening when students complain about disrespectful or hostile speech may be an expedient way to avoid student protest and encourage civility, but it is clearly untenable. Many current practices by campus officials appear to violate the Constitution. In fact, an analysis of 466 universities conducted by the Foundation for Individual Rights and Expression (FIRE) in 2020 found that only 50 institutions were in full compliance with the First Amendment.[9]

Amid this confusion, surveys of faculty and student opinion reveal that confidence in academic freedom on most college campuses has deteriorated over recent decades. Whereas surveys in 1969 found that more than three-quarters of the faculty in American universities agreed that "the administration of your university supports academic freedom," the percentage fell to 55 percent in 1999 and dropped again to 41 percent by 2007.[10] The percentage of professors claiming that their own academic freedom had been threatened reached 28 percent in 2007, a figure even higher than was recorded during the McCarthy period in the late 1940s and early 1950s.[11] The percentage is perhaps even higher today. Greg Lukianoff, president of FIRE, declared in 2020 that "academic freedom is in the worst position of my career, and perhaps the worst condition it has been in decades."[12] In an article in 2020 in the *Atlantic,* John McWhorter, a Columbia professor, claimed that "the majority of my fellow instructors and staff constantly self-censor themselves in fear of being fired for expressing the wrong opinions."[13] Students, especially those with conservative views, are likewise reluctant to express their opinions on controversial subjects. Legitimate topics for discussion, such as those having to do with race, gender, or sexual orientation, can become minefields that students and professors hesitate to enter for fear that some innocent remark will subject them to condemnation, public embarrassment, and, in the case of faculty, even endanger their career.

A DIFFERENT APPROACH

The University of Chicago has chosen a different way to deal with these issues. A committee of professors appointed by the president issued a report on free speech in 2015 that has since been endorsed by scores of other universities, including Princeton, Johns Hopkins, Purdue, and the University of Wisconsin.[14] The following excerpts from the report convey the essence of its message:

> Because the University is committed to free and open inquiry in all matters, it guarantees all members of the University community the broadest possible latitude to speak, write, listen, challenge, and learn. . . .
> Of course, the ideas of different members of the University community will often and quite naturally conflict. But it is not the proper

role of the University to attempt to shield individuals from ideas and opinions they find unwelcome, disagreeable, or even deeply offensive.

The report goes on to point out:

Although the University greatly values civility, and although all members of the University community share in the responsibility for maintaining a climate of mutual respect, concerns about civility and mutual respect can never be used as a justification for closing off discussion of ideas, however offensive or disagreeable those ideas may be to some members of the community. . . . As a corollary to the University's commitment to protect and promote free expression, members of the University community must also act in conformity with the principle of free expression. Although members of the University community are free to criticize and contest the views expressed on campus, and to criticize and contest speakers who are invited to express their views on campus, they may not obstruct or otherwise interfere with the freedom of others to express views they reject or even loathe.

The committee did recognize that there are legal limits to the right to speak freely. "The University may restrict expression that violates the law, that falsely defames a specific individual, that constitutes a genuine threat or harassment, that unjustifiably invades substantial privacy or confidentiality interests, or that is otherwise directly incompatible with the functioning of the University." But, the committee added, "these are narrow exceptions to the general principle of freedom of expression, and it is vitally important that these exceptions never be used in a manner that is inconsistent with the University's commitment to a completely free and open discussion of ideas."

This statement does a lot to clarify the meaning of free speech on the Chicago campus. Instructors, whether or not they have tenure, can feel confident that they will not be subject to discipline or have their career at the university endangered for expressing ideas and arguments that some consider offensive. Students can expect that those who disrupt speeches will be disciplined and that the university will not require trigger warnings or take action to protect them from listening to professors who utter statements they find offensive.

The extensive protection that the Chicago committee has afforded to speech and ideas is generally in accord with my own beliefs. Nevertheless, the statement barely touches on how a university should respond to an extreme case of speech so flagrantly hateful and malicious that it is bound to injure the feelings of those whom it disparages without containing any ideas or information of any redeeming value. Moreover, although the Chicago statement makes a cursory reference to the legitimate need to provide a civil, welcoming, and inclusive environment for all students, it does not explain how this objective can be achieved without impinging on the broad protection for speech set forth in the rest of the statement. Thus, the Chicago manifesto by itself does not give much help to harried campus officials wondering what they can do to uphold freedom of speech and still maintain a reasonably civil, supportive, and welcoming environment for all members of their increasingly diverse student body.[15]

RESOLVING THE DILEMMA

How, then, can a university reconcile both of these worthy but conflicting goals? My own view is that the administration should begin by issuing a well-publicized statement similar to the Chicago declaration to avoid the confusion that has currently obscured the status of freedom of speech on many campuses. Such a statement should be accompanied by a detailed exposition of the reasons why such freedom is essential to the mission of a university.

These steps are admittedly insufficient by themselves to convince minority students and other offended groups that the university truly respects their feelings and welcomes their presence on the campus. What more, then, can the administration do to respond to these concerns?

A crucial first step in dealing with speech that may offend or disparage vulnerable groups of students is to be clear about what goal the university is trying to pursue. Does it simply wish to protect minorities and identity groups from disrespectful speech and hostile behavior, or does it prefer the larger goal of encouraging the widest possible exchange of civil argument and discussion? The latter goal has much to recommend it. It is evenhanded in recognizing that uncivil and demeaning speech can be directed at conservative students as well as at racial minorities and LGBTQ individuals. Moreover, by choosing this wider objective, the university minimizes the risk of emphasizing one of these objectives and paying insufficient attention to the other. What follows is an effort to describe specifically what this broader effort would entail.

To implement a policy that combines a desire not only to support and welcome students who may feel most vulnerable but also to encourage civil discourse about controversial issues, universities need to select a staff that has experience in the pursuit of both objectives. If the mission of Diversity, Equity, and Inclusion is conceived and staffed entirely as a group to protect the interests of ethnic minorities and LGBTQ students, the effort will run a continuing risk of ignoring the free speech protections for all students and faculty and adopting measures such as issuing long lists of allegedly insensitive words that go to absurd lengths, inhibit people from speaking, and often invite ridicule on the entire DEI initiative.

Student Speech

Although the First Amendment properly gives great latitude to faculty and students to express even the most distasteful thoughts and ideas, it does not prevent a university president, or anyone else, from expressing disagreement with what has been said. In flagrant cases of disrespect for others, the administration has not only a right but a responsibility to make its disagreement known in unequivocal terms.

Although official expressions of disagreement are needed in flagrant cases of disrespectful or hateful speech, they will not suffice to reassure the victims of such behavior if they are not backed up by the actions and policies of the university. As most institutions have come to realize, many women and minorities will not feel welcome and fully accepted unless their place in the university is recognized not only by its admissions policies but also by appropriate courses in the curriculum and by the appointment of qualified women and minorities to positions in the faculty and administration. Many colleges have already done a great deal to accomplish this result. Every college should be able to do so, since the numbers of women and minorities with the education and experience to qualify for such appointments are much larger today than they were fifty years ago, when college authorities first recognized the need to diversify their faculties and staffs.

Universities can also conduct voluntary workshops for faculty and students on issues involving race and gender and the ways in which individuals can unwittingly give offense or exhibit prejudice against particular groups of students. Properly conducted, such programs have been shown to be beneficial.[16] At the same time, great care must be taken to encourage frank discussion and avoid seeming to indoctrinate the audience or leave students feeling unfairly accused of being bigoted.*

College administrators can also encourage student governments, campus newspapers, and other undergraduate organizations to speak out when flagrant examples of prejudice occur, not by shaming the speaker but by expressing their support for a diverse campus community where students from all races and backgrounds and sexual orientations are welcome and respected. Those who utter disparaging remarks as well as those who have been maligned will often be more influenced by the opinions of their peers than by official statements from the administration. Since surveys repeatedly show widespread support on most campuses for a diverse and inclusive student body, prominent student groups should be willing to help reassure the victims of hostile behavior and others like them that the offensive statements of some undergraduates do not reflect the attitudes of the student body as a whole.

At the same time, much controversial speech on campus is not hostile or disrespectful toward minorities, women, or other identity groups. On the contrary, it may consist of efforts to shame or disparage individuals who have expressed views that are thought to be racist or prejudiced in some other way. Often, the criticism conveys no more than vehement disagreement with another student's

*There is a tendency on some campuses when staffing offices of equity and inclusion to pay more attention to choosing individuals with a strong commitment to overcoming racial or LGBTQ prejudice than to determining whether the applicants have sufficient knowledge of and commitment to freedom of speech. This tendency naturally creates a risk that educational programs and other efforts to promote understanding and respect will fail to pay sufficient attention to upholding the First Amendment. By doing so, universities can have the opposite effect on students from the one they are trying to foster. See, e.g., Adam S. Hoffman, "My Liberal Campus Is Pushing Free Thinkers to the Right," guest essay, *New York Times,* March 1, 2023.

opinion on a sensitive topic. Even so, many students self-censor, because they are reluctant to express unpopular views that may provoke disapproval by their classmates on a variety of sensitive subjects such as politics, race, and gender.[17] Instructors cannot prevent such reactions, but they can at least encourage students with unpopular views to speak up and engage in a discussion.

Students are not the only ones responsible for creating an atmosphere of political correctness or "cancel culture." There are organizations outside the university that unleash torrents of abuse through social media on faculty members or students who express whatever these groups regard as biased or offensive views. Such tactics are unfortunate. Nevertheless, while campus officials can issue statements reassuring aggrieved students and faculty that they disapprove of shaming or threatening messages, universities have no power to punish such behavior or remove the harm they cause.

Despite the efforts of campus officials to respond to hostile and bigoted speech, conversations and other behaviors by individuals continue to occur on every campus that seem unfriendly to minority students or to women, gays, or other groups by appearing to question their intelligence or even their presence in the university. Minority students report receiving more than twice as many of these "microaggressive" communications as White students do. Many of the remarks may be unintentional or misunderstood. Still, they tend to counteract the efforts of universities to make women, minorities, first-generation students, and other "different" groups feel fully welcome and comfortable. Once again, however, unless the speech involved meets the narrow definition of harassment articulated by the Supreme Court, universities cannot punish the speaker under the First Amendment and could not prevent such random, informal behavior even if they tried.

Rather than punishing students who utter hostile or disrespectful views, campus authorities can speak with blatant offenders to try to make them understand how harmful their words can be to the feelings of the victims and the climate of decency and civility that the university is trying to maintain. Properly done, such efforts are often more effective than punishment in changing the behavior of the perpetrators.

Faculty Speech

Different problems arise in protecting the rights of faculty members to express their opinions on controversial subjects. The extent of protection for speech by faculty members, both in the classroom and elsewhere, is still unclear, especially for professors who make statements that seem insensitive or disrespectful to minorities, gays, or other student groups.

The current situation on many campuses is unfortunate. Newspapers publish a constant trickle of reports about instructors who have been investigated, temporarily suspended, or fired for statements that are ambiguous or even accurate but have given rise to heated student protest. As I previously noted, one professor was suspended, investigated, and subsequently asked to withdraw from teaching a course in which he showed a film starring Laurence Olivier in blackface. Another instructor had to resign simply for referring to the COVID-19 virus as the "Chinese virus."

At still another well-known university, a private conversation between two adjunct professors was accidentally recorded in which one of the instructors remarked: "I end up having this angst every semester that a lot of my [lower-performing] ones are Blacks. Happens almost every semester. And it is like, oh, come on. You get some really good ones. But there are also usually some that are just plain at the bottom. It drives me crazy."[18]

These remarks, though none too clear, do not strike me as plainly hostile, biased, or even factually inaccurate. Nevertheless, the tape was subsequently discovered, whereupon a large number of students and professors protested and urged the speaker's removal. She was subsequently fired by the dean, who called her remarks "reprehensible statements concerning the evaluation of Black students" and "illustrative of the conscious and unconscious bias systemic in law school grading." This action seems in direct conflict with the First Amendment and the university's own stated policy "to provide all members of the University community, including faculty, students, and staff, the broadest possible latitude to speak, write, listen, challenge, and learn."

As incidents such as these continue to be widely publicized, many professors are bound to feel inhibited from speaking on sensitive topics both in and outside the classroom for fear that they will arouse a controversy that could endanger their careers. Such conditions stifle legitimate discussion and make it all the more necessary for campus leaders to recognize the danger and try to dispel it by issuing clear statements affirming their commitment to a free and vigorous expression of ideas and instructing officials throughout the university to abide by this policy.

The task of building confidence among the faculty about their right to speak freely is complicated by the concomitant need to discourage attempts on the part of instructors to indoctrinate their students. The concept of academic freedom as defined by the American Association of University Professors is quite clear on the rights and responsibilities of professors' speech in the classroom.[19] Instructors must be free to express their opinions in class, but only if they do not amount to indoctrination and are germane to the subject matter of the course. This guideline seems to be violated with disturbing frequency. In a survey in 2018, a large majority of students reported that they had taken classes in which the professor expressed personal opinions on politics and other matters unrelated to the course.[20] Over half of these students indicated that such expressions of opinion happened "often," while many more replied that they had "sometimes" but "not often" encountered such instructors.

One can argue that there is no need to worry about the expression of unrelated political opinions. Such views, by definition, have nothing to do with the course, so that students need not feel constrained to pay attention to, much less agree with, them. Even so, the prevalence of such remarks by instructors not only wastes the time of students but may strengthen the impression shared by many conservatives that college faculties frequently indoctrinate students with their liberal orthodoxies.* While extraneous expressions of opinion in the classroom should not warrant disciplinary action, professors have no reason to complain if campus authorities privately urge them to try to avoid such digressions in their teaching, especially if their opinions are political or of a highly controversial nature.

More difficult questions arise over how an administration should respond to complaints about expressions of opinion by professors that give offense to a particular group of students.

---

*I am also troubled by the implication that professors should feel free to express their opinions in class provided they *are* relevant to the subject matter of the course. This principle would appear to give free rein to professors of political science to express views on politics or to offer their personal opinions on all kinds of controversial questions germane to the subject they are teaching. Many students in the course are bound to feel that they should not contradict these opinions in the papers and exams they write out of fear that that their grades will suffer as a result. Critics who claim that liberal professors indoctrinate their students will believe with some reason that such behavior gives proof for their concerns. All things considered, then, it would seem better for instructors to encourage students to think for themselves about the solutions to controversial issues.

Although the principles of academic freedom protect the right of professors to speak their mind on matters within their field of expertise, the First Amendment gives instructors in public universities the right to express their opinions on any subject outside the classroom no matter how distasteful or unpopular their views may be. There is no reason why private universities should employ a different standard. Stanford, for example, did not penalize its Nobel physicist William B. Shockley even though he repeatedly expressed his opinion that Blacks were inferior in intelligence to Whites. Once again, instead of taking punitive actions against professors who express unpopular views, academic leaders should simply make clear to offended students that the controversial views of particular professors are not shared by the university.

A more troublesome question for universities is how to respond to students who do not demand that any instructor be fired but claim that they should not be forced to learn from professors who have expressed views either in or outside the classroom that the students regard as upsetting or abhorrent. In recent years, activist students have frequently combed the writings of instructors and their entries on Google, Facebook, and Twitter to find expressions of opinion that they consider deeply offensive. They have then made these findings public and demanded that the professors be prevented from teaching.

A few public universities appear to have terminated or rescinded the appointments of instructors who have expressed such views, an action that seems plainly wrong and in violation of First Amendment principles. More often, however, universities have responded not by firing the instructors or docking their pay, but by suspending them from teaching during an investigation and then persuading them to withdraw from the course or providing alternative sections of the course taught by instructors who will not make students uncomfortable. In one case, when a tenured law professor gave an exam question about a trial in which a hypothetical prosecutor was said to refer to another woman as a "b——" and a "n——," the professor was actually suspended from teaching and forced to complete a reeducation program comprising lectures, tutorials, and required essays describing what he had learned. Other universities have even rebuked instructors in literature courses for reading passages by well-known authors that included "sensitive" words.

One can understand why zealous campus officials might be tempted to resolve an angry student complaint in this way. Yet doing so will come at a cost. If professors know that anything they have ever written or said in class that offends their students may lead to investigations by their university and possible removal from a course or loss of students to an alternative version of their class, they are likely to become excessively cautious about what they say and even refuse to teach any class in which they will have to discuss sensitive issues.

Campus leaders and their staffs have other ways to demonstrate the university's commitment to a diverse student body and a welcoming and supportive environment for all who are enrolled. If the views expressed by a faculty member are clearly not consistent with this policy, academic leaders can express their disagreement with the instructor in order to reassure the students. But conducting lengthy investigations and providing alternative classes can humiliate the teacher and afford greater protection and reassurance than the aggrieved students need or deserve. On this point, Hanna Gray's observation seems especially apt: "Education should not be intended to make people comfortable, it is meant to make them think."[21] If a university means to prepare its students for life in the real world, it cannot shield them from contact with every instructor who expresses, or has ever expressed, an opinion or a word that they regard as insensitive or disrespectful.

THE BOTTOM LINE

There is much to regret about the current conflict between free speech and the effort to build a tolerant and civil environment. Both sides in this debate have the best of intentions. The staunch defenders of free speech are striving to uphold a foundational value essential to the mission of the university to search for truth and understanding. At the same time, the effort to promote "diversity, equity, and inclusion" is inspired by a laudable desire for civility, decency, and tolerance, conditions that are also important for achieving the goals of every educational institution. In these circumstances, the appropriate aim for campus leaders should not be to choose one side over the other but to look for a viable way to pursue both objectives simultaneously.

It will not do to try to accomplish this goal by proclaiming a commitment to uphold free speech while ignoring it when necessary to satisfy students aggrieved over some intemperate or disrespectful remark. On the contrary, if one of the goals involved must be abandoned to achieve the other, there is good reason not to sacrifice freedom of speech. From a legal standpoint, only free speech is explicitly guaranteed by the Constitution, while civility and mutual respect are not. If universities abandon liberty of speech to appease disgruntled students, the result will be to create confusion among the faculty about the extent of their freedom to express their opinions, produce resentment among students at being disciplined for their beliefs, and bring disapproval from their critics for ignoring the First Amendment.

At the same time, the primacy of free speech need not and should not simply call for a tolerance of hostile or demeaning speech so long as it does not convey an immediate threat of violence or take the form of sustained harassment. Rather, big-oted or abusive speech on campus should be met with efforts by the administration to reassure the offended students of the university's support and, where appropriate, with an attempt to explain to the perpetrators why their behavior is hurtful and in conflict with the values of the university.

The attempt to reconcile free speech with the desire for civility and mutual respect is admittedly hard to carry out success-fully. It is difficult to change the minds of bigots or to satisfy angry students who feel demeaned and disrespected. In the end, however, the approach suggested here is the only one that tries to serve both of the essential values at stake when cases of hostile or disrespectful speech roil the campus.

PART IV

———

Beyond the Ideological Divide

ALTHOUGH THE ISSUES RAISED BY LIBERALS AND conservatives have attracted much attention in recent years, they are not the only, or even the most important, problems confronting the nation's elite universities. The chapters in Part 4 seek to complete this study by discussing some of these often-overlooked problems.

Chapter 9 examines the quality of undergraduate education provided by elite universities. As I pointed out in chapter 1, elites need to make a particular effort to achieve several goals because of the exceptional abilities of their students and the likelihood that many of their alumni will have careers of consequence to many others. Specifically, they should take particular care to help their undergraduates choose careers, prepare them to be active and informed citizens, and develop their ability to perceive and think carefully about the ethical questions they encounter in their later lives. There is little evidence that our leading universities are meeting these responsibilities as well as they should. Chapter 9 seeks to explain why they have not made greater progress and what their academic leaders might do to improve on the current record.

Chapter 10 takes up the long-standing problem of reconciling intercollegiate athletics with basic academic values and draws on my personal experience to explain why overcoming these problems is all but impossible for the great athletic powers that attract so much of the attention (and the revenue) generated by college sports. Most elite universities are not great athletic powers, however, and have a greater chance of bringing their programs into closer conformity with appropriate academic principles. Much of the chapter is devoted to exploring the prospects for achieving this goal and the obstacles that stand in the way.

Finally, chapter 11 examines three trends that are already creating difficulty for leading universities and promise to get worse as time goes on: the tendency for every segment of the university to organize and demand a seat at the table to bargain over questions that could affect their interests; the problems caused by the insatiable need to raise more and more money; and last, the tendency of governments to regulate more and more subjects that were long considered academic matters to be resolved by universities themselves. I provide no answers for these difficult trends since I cannot think of any feasible solutions to offer. Even so, I discuss the problems in the hope that wiser heads than mine may discover ways to resolve them.

_____

CHAPTER 9

Should Our Leading Universities Do More to Improve the Quality of Education?

IN THE DECADES FOLLOWING THE CIVIL WAR, A HANDFUL of institutions, notably Cornell, Chicago, Harvard, and Johns Hopkins, led the way in introducing reforms that emphasized research and the training of scientists and scholars, improved the education of undergraduates, and eventually gave rise to the first modern research universities in America. Today, however, when one reads about the leaders in improving higher education, the names of institutions such as Arizona State, Southern New Hampshire, and Georgia State regularly appear, while neither members of the Ivy League nor other elite universities are mentioned.

One reason elite institutions never get cited for their innovations in undergraduate education is that most of the successful reforms in recent years have involved widely recognized problems such as high dropout rates and unaffordable tuitions that our most prominent universities do not have. There is one important problem, however, that elites do share with most other colleges and universities. A growing body of evidence suggests that the quality of undergraduate education in America is not what it should be and that students may not even be learning as much as they did several decades ago.

Students today appear to be spending much less time than they once did on preparing for class.[1] Although faculties repeatedly rate critical thinking as the most important goal of undergraduate education, one prominent study has revealed that college students make only modest progress toward mastering this skill, while other studies find that their competence has actually declined over the last thirty years.[2] Elite colleges seem to be doing a bit better. Nevertheless, despite the steady growth in the number of courses in their catalogues, the many amenities they offer their students, and the wide array of extracurricular activities they provide, I doubt that many elite colleges have adequately fulfilled their responsibility to help their students decide how they wish to use their talents in later life. Moreover, notwithstanding the growing threats to our democracy and the loss of confidence in almost all major American institutions, there is little indication that elites have done all that they could and should to prepare undergraduates adequately to be active and engaged citizens, or to develop their capacity to perceive ethical issues when they arise and to think carefully about how to resolve them.*

*While professional schools rarely include courses on civic education in their curricula, most do provide extensive opportunities for interested students to engage in service activities or pro bono groups that assist individuals in need of professional help. With the encouragement of the organized bar, law schools, including the leading schools, have gone further to incorporate such activities in the curriculum as a way both to teach their students lawyerly skills and encourage them to develop habits of pro bono legal service as a normal part of professional life. Professional schools also appear to be doing more than colleges to require courses on ethics. Alumni and professional organizations have pressed them to do so. As a result, law schools and almost all leading business and medical schools have courses on professional ethics. A number of business schools have reported difficulty getting students interested in the courses or persuading them that ethical responsibility is a part of becoming a competent professional. More recently, however, several leading schools have introduced promising courses on the social responsibilities of corporations.

WHY CREATING AN APPROPRIATE CURRICULUM
IS SO DIFFICULT FOR ELITE UNIVERSITIES

Ironically, many of these deficiencies have their roots in the great advances made by America's colleges and universities during the decades following the Civil War. These reforms were often inspired by the much-admired German universities, but there was one important feature of America's transformation that did not follow the German model. In Germany, postsecondary education and research were kept largely separate. Leading scientists and scholars were appointed to chairs in independent institutes where they could conduct their experiments, write their books, and mentor the next generation of research specialists. In the United States, however, scientists and scholars remained responsible for teaching undergraduates in addition to carrying on their research and training graduate students for academic careers.

The American system has had several advantages. It has allowed undergraduates in our leading universities to learn from the most accomplished experts in each field of study. In addition, by teaching undergraduates, these distinguished thinkers have had to adjust their specialized knowledge to fit a younger, unspecialized, less knowledgeable audience, which may have helped keep them from becoming excessively narrow in their own work.

At the same time, combining research and undergraduate teaching has disadvantages that have become more serious over the intervening decades, as the tenured faculty has gained near-total control over the content of the undergraduate curriculum and the methods of instruction. Since teaching college students is only one of the faculty's several duties, it must compete for the time and attention of professors with graduate (PhD) training and research. These multiple duties have important consequences for undergraduate education.

Because the quality of research contributes most to the reputation of their university, new members of the faculty in leading universities are appointed and rewarded for their success as scientists and scholars more than for their ability as teachers and educators. The emphasis on published research in choosing professors and the dominance of the research-oriented faculty in determining matters of educational policy have in turn had important effects on the undergraduate curriculum. Even in the early decades of the twentieth century, when the basic structure of the modern undergraduate curriculum first took shape, decisions about the teaching program were deliberately made to accommodate the emerging research-oriented faculty. The extensive use of lectures was encouraged because it made fewer demands on professors than more active methods of teaching, thus giving them more time for research. The requirement that students complete a specialized college major, the ample number of electives, and the prevalence of distribution requirements all enabled professors to offer instruction in their own specialized field of expertise and limited the use of required courses that could force them and their colleagues to teach less familiar subjects that would demand more time for preparation and interest them less.

Throughout the ensuing decades, faculties have continued to preserve these advantages and resist reforms that could force them to spend more time preparing to teach required courses or mastering innovative methods of instruction. Thus, almost all of the improvements in undergraduate education that have occurred over the past seventy-five years—such as the growth of international courses, freshman seminars, ethnic and women's studies programs, teaching and learning centers, and online courses—have been initiatives that could be staffed by hiring new instructors without having to persuade professors to teach courses outside their chosen specialized fields.

For these reasons, the periodic faculty reviews of the curriculum seldom include much discussion on how to give all students an adequate civic education or help them improve their ethical awareness and moral reasoning. Mandatory courses are usually disliked by students and could force a number of professors to teach one of the many sections of these classes that would be needed to reach the entire student body. As a result, many faculties feel that discussing such requirements would be fruitless.

There is also little discussion during faculty reviews of the curriculum concerning topics such as whether students should be allowed so many electives, or whether they need to take so many courses in their major in order to learn how to explore a subject in depth, or whether distribution requirements (which simply require students to choose at least one or two existing courses from each of several large categories) are truly the best or even a sensible way to give students the desired "breadth" of a liberal education. All these questions are well worth considering, but each of them threatens to call for changes that could limit the freedom of professors to choose the courses they teach and to continue giving specialized classes and seminars that match their current research interests.

Because the basic structure of the curriculum serves the interests of the faculty so well, it has remained largely intact for more than one hundred years. The periodic reviews of the undergraduate program are usually confined to tinkering with the few general education courses that are left after the field of concentration (that is, the major), student electives, and distribution requirements have all claimed their accustomed place in the teaching program. Since members of the tenured faculty can normally feel quite confident that their vital interests will be protected, fewer than half of them in many elite universities bother to attend the review meetings or vote on recommended changes to the curriculum.

Over the years, the multiple responsibilities of the tenured faculty have also led them to reduce the number of courses they teach and to delegate many of the less agreeable forms of teaching to other kinds of instructors. Small discussion sections of lecture courses have long been entrusted to graduate (PhD) students, along with much of the burdensome task of grading papers and exams. Elementary courses, such as introductory classes in writing, mathematics, and foreign languages, have become the responsibility of graduate students or untenured lecturers. More recently, non-tenure-track instructors, often hired on annual appointments, have been used in increasing numbers to teach introductory and general education courses. In all, instructors who are not on the tenure track now make up an average of at least half and often two-thirds of all the teachers of undergraduates in most colleges and universities. As a result of these changes, the average teaching load of professors in leading universities has dropped substantially in recent decades.

To be fair, there are many outstanding tenured scientists and scholars who still teach large undergraduate courses, love doing so, and are very good at it. In fact, 40 percent of all tenure-track professors in research universities claim that they are more interested in teaching than research.[3] But there are also many others who have perfected the art of teaching the necessary number of credit hours each week with few enough students and sufficiently little effort to leave them ample time for research, mentoring graduate students, committee assignments, and other administrative responsibilities.

Deans and other academic leaders have accepted this system not only because they have little power to prevent it but also because it has the virtue of being relatively inexpensive.

The adjunct lecturers and graduate students who now make up more than half of all undergraduate teachers cost much less money than tenure-track professors. Since many of them are hired on one-year appointments and can be terminated on little or no notice, deans can increase or decrease their number quite quickly and thus adjust more easily to fluctuations in the financial condition of the university. As a result, during times of serious budgetary pressure, many deans and provosts have appreciated the chance to gain flexibility and save money by hiring non-tenure-track instructors to replace retiring tenured faculty.

Under these conditions, the incentives for experimenting with new and better methods of teaching are very weak. Students are not clamoring for reform. Nor are there any financial benefits for universities from introducing more effective methods of teaching. As a result, the process of improving teaching and learning is sluggish at best.

The most obvious example of this tendency is the snail-like transition from relying heavily on lecturing to a passive student audience to a pedagogy emphasizing active discussion and problem solving. The drawbacks of lecturing have been known for well over a century. President Eliot put the matter well in his inaugural address in 1869: "The lecturer pumps laboriously into sieves. The water may be wholesome, but it runs through. A mind must work to grow."[4]

Despite this warning, the transition to more active learning has been extremely slow. Eliot himself came to accept lecturing because it demanded less effort by professors and left them more time to pursue their research. Now that a substantial body of empirical research has revealed the superiority of discussion and problem solving for developing critical thinking, these methods of instruction have become more common. Still, according to a faculty survey in 2017 of undergraduate teaching throughout the

United States, 51 percent of the respondents reported making extensive use of lecturing.[5]*

It is easy to criticize the slow pace of reform as a simple case of powerful professors neglecting their responsibility to students. My years of observing the system, however, have led me to dismiss this explanation as too facile. There is little evidence that most tenured professors in elite research universities are shirking their responsibilities. By all accounts, they continue to devote well over forty hours per week to their work—significantly above the average for faculty members in any other type of college or university.[6] During times when classes are in session, most professors spend far more time on teaching than they do on their research. Contrary to what some critics have charged, the vast majority of tenured professors, even in research-intensive universities, spend no more than an hour or two per week on consulting or other outside activities. It is therefore likely that the unwillingness to embrace time-consuming reforms is actually a defensible way to accommodate the multiple responsibilities of professors. In view of the research accomplishments of these universities, the huge demand for admission to their colleges, and the exceptionally high satisfaction of their alumni with their undergraduate education, it is hard to make a convincing case that their faculties are selfishly refusing to devote enough effort to teaching undergraduates. After all, tenured faculty in elite universities are expected

*The role of lectures in professional schools has varied markedly. In law schools, the Socratic method was introduced in the late nineteenth century and has remained the principal method of teaching law students ever since. In medical schools, lecturing continued to be the primary method for teaching first-year students until the 1980s but has since ceded pride of place to small-group problem solving in most schools. In business schools, the practice varies from a predominant reliance on discussion using elaborate cases from actual companies in some schools to a much heavier use of lecturing in others.

to make important discoveries and write books that enrich their field of knowledge while simultaneously teaching undergraduates and mentoring graduate students to eventually become leaders in their chosen subject. Asking these professors to do even more by mastering a new method of instruction or teaching a section of a compulsory course on moral reasoning or civic education must surely be a bridge too far.

Under these conditions, there is little prospect for improving the quality of undergraduate education by simply urging the tenured faculty to make major changes in the curriculum or the way they teach their students. At best, academic leaders can improve the incentives for experimenting with new and better methods of instruction by disseminating information about promising ways to improve student learning and by providing individual professors with the extra time, the funds, and the technical assistance to try new methods if they are interested in doing so. These inducements, however, will seldom succeed in persuading professors to accept reforms that could require them to offer courses they do not care to teach or commit them to fundamental changes in their methods of instruction that could take too much time from their research. They may agree to such steps if the evidence for doing so is compelling; consider the immediate shift to teaching by Zoom and other forms of distance learning during the coronavirus pandemic. But the evidence for making major changes in pedagogy or introducing compulsory courses to meet important educational needs is rarely strong enough to make a compelling case for faculty approval.

Because of the collective reluctance to consider major changes in the undergraduate program, there is a wide gap between the way professors in leading universities describe the goals of a college education and the effort with which these goals are actually being pursued. Eighty percent or more of faculty members say they believe that college should teach students to reason critically, to become active and informed citizens, to acquire personal values and a philosophy of life, and to develop a stronger, more informed ability to behave ethically.[7] Yet faculties spend remarkably little time and effort discovering how much progress students are actually making toward these goals or how they might be taught to learn more. Such empirical evidence as exists suggests that the improvement students make is considerably less than most professors think, even in elite universities, and may in some cases have diminished over the last several decades.[8]

Another sign of the sluggish pace of reform in undergraduate teaching is the casual treatment given to expanding the aims of undergraduate education to embrace new and important forms of learning. In recent years, psychologists, most of whom are faculty members in leading universities, have discovered that important qualities of mind and behavior that were long believed to be fixed and immutable by early childhood actually continue to develop throughout the traditional college years and hence are potentially teachable.[9]

These discoveries could give rise to a new and important step in the evolution of college teaching by developing valuable capabilities and qualities of mind such as empathy, creativity, conscientiousness, and teamwork that could enrich the lives of students and enhance their value to employers. Thus far, however, there is little sign of any concerted effort by elite colleges to pursue these possibilities. Research on how to develop these qualities of mind has not proceeded very far, and much of the work is insufficiently rigorous, sample sizes are often too small, controls are frequently missing, and other important details are sometimes absent. While courses that seek to teach these subjects are being taught on many campuses, most of the courses are taught by instructors who are not on the tenure track, and

their efforts have not received much attention or encouragement from the permanent faculty or the college administration.
The casual effort to develop ways to teach these capabilities
provides a striking contrast with the strenuous efforts made by
many large corporations to develop new products and improve
existing ones. The difference presumably results from the fact
that new and improved commercial products are an important
source of profit for corporations, while more effective ways of
teaching rarely bring similar rewards to universities.

SOME FEASIBLE WAYS TO ENCOURAGE REFORM

Despite the obstacles that impede the process of educational
reform, there are several steps that academic leaders could take
that would speed the process of improving the quality of education without much risk of encountering serious faculty opposition.

Research

One such initiative for presidents to use would be to develop a
stronger in-house program of research to discover better ways
of measuring progress in student learning with which to identify
weaknesses in existing programs and evaluate new and potentially improved methods of instruction. Reliable evidence that
students are not learning as much as they should, and that more
effective methods of teaching exist, is essential to convince a
skeptical faculty that reform is needed.

The use of credible data to reform teaching, however, is limited
not only by the reluctance of many professors to discover how
much their students are learning but by the lack of widely accepted
tests for measuring progress. There are adequate methods for testing competence in reading and speaking foreign languages and
solving problems in mathematics and science. Promising tests have
also been developed for measuring the ability to analyze practical

problems or even reason about moral dilemmas. Interest has grown in developing rubrics that describe the stages of growth in achieving learning objectives that can then be used to evaluate students' work and determine how much they are progressing, although grading rubrics may be too slow and arduous a process to be widely used. Suitable ways of measuring competence are even harder to find in the humanities and harder still for evaluating qualities of mind and behavior such as creativity and empathy.* It can be difficult in some fields even to reach agreement on the meaning of critical thinking, let alone measure students' progress in mastering this method of thought. Even if reliable tests of student progress are developed, it can be hard to make sure that students will try to do their best on tests that do not count toward their final grade.

Though some of the research needed to overcome these problems may be done by interested members of the faculty, much of the effort will not materialize without a larger and stronger in-house staff and a substantially increased budget. Several universities already seem to be moving in this direction by creating centers for innovation in teaching. Through greater efforts of this kind, leading universities may eventually follow the successful example of pharmaceutical companies and other large commercial enterprises in America that have long devoted substantial amounts of money and research to a continuous effort to improve the quality of what they do.

*Even so, many of these behaviors are already being taught to interested students in a number of colleges. Some of this teaching is done by regular members of the tenure-track faculty. More often, however, the courses are taught by instructors who are not faculty members but administrative personnel in offices such as career counseling, student affairs, or health services. Such courses are tolerated, but the instructors have no voice in deliberations about the goals and content of undergraduate education, and their teaching is seldom encouraged or evaluated carefully by the faculty to determine its effectiveness.

Improving Graduate (PhD) Training

Another way for elite universities to increase student learning involves the training of graduate students who plan to seek an academic career. Over one hundred years have passed since William James criticized the failure of PhD programs to prepare their students to teach.[10] Since then, some important improvements have been made, but they tend to be voluntary and are often lacking in adequate support and involvement from the tenured faculty.

For many years, professors argued that such preparation was unnecessary because teaching was a highly personal activity that could best be developed through experience and practice rather than formal training. Today, however, several developments have combined to make formal preparation more necessary. The growing body of knowledge about how students learn, coupled with the expanding use of technology to enhance instruction, calls for competencies that tomorrow's teachers cannot easily acquire without some form of instruction. It is all the more important to supply this preparation now that more and more newly graduated PhDs from leading universities are finding faculty positions in colleges where teaching undergraduates is the sole or primary task of the faculty.

While formal training in teaching and learning has become more important, most departments are not equipped to meet the need, because their members are rarely well acquainted with all of the relevant knowledge that future college teachers need to acquire. Thus, a vacuum exists that only the administration can fill by working with departments to marshal the necessary expertise from existing teaching and learning centers and from elsewhere in the university to help departments provide the kinds of instruction that future faculty members require.

Faculties may initially resist such a reform on the ground that graduate education has always been the business of departments. They may argue that additional training is unnecessary or insist that it would be unwise since graduate students already take too long to earn their degree. Academic leaders, however, have various ways to overcome such resistance.

Since the administration provides the funds to pay graduate students for their teaching, it has some power to insist on minimum standards. During my tenure as president, I encountered no resistance when I insisted that graduate students from foreign countries pass a qualifying oral test to ensure that they could speak English adequately. Moreover, when I sought to prevent any graduate student who received especially poor student evaluations from teaching without completing a course provided by our teaching and learning center, I also encountered no objection from the faculty.

Many of the teaching and learning centers that exist in research universities already offer useful programs and services for helping interested graduate students. Such training can be made more attractive by offering graduate students who complete a certain amount of preparation a certificate of their accomplishment that could help them find a faculty position after they graduate. If the training is well designed and helps new PhDs with their careers, departments will be less likely to resist making it an accepted part of the graduate program, especially since doing so will not require the tenured faculty to alter their behavior or take time from their research.

The Role of Non-Tenure-Track Faculty

A final opportunity for leading universities involves the increasing use of non-tenure-track instructors to teach undergraduates. By now, these teachers outnumber the tenured faculty in most research universities. Their treatment leaves much to be desired. They are often hired haphazardly without anything like the care routinely taken in hiring tenure-track professors. They typically receive low pay and few if any of the usual benefits. Many are employed on a year-to-year basis, can be terminated without notice, and have no voice or vote in faculty discussions of undergraduate education.

A number of studies have found that the extensive use of part-time adjunct faculty can have adverse effects on the quality of education.[11] Often juggling several jobs, these instructors tend to have less time than tenure-track faculty for preparing their courses or talking informally with students. They are also more inclined to lecture rather than use more active methods of learning and to give short-answer tests instead of essay exams. Several researchers have even found that extensive use of untrained adjunct teachers tends to result in higher numbers of students who drop out.[12]

The heavy use of non-tenure-track instructors and the shabby treatment they receive are an embarrassment for universities. Recent surveys find that substantial majorities of tenured professors recognize this problem and support improving the salaries and working conditions of these instructors and even giving them a vote in faculty reviews of the undergraduate program.[13] Nevertheless, the financial problems faced by many colleges and universities make them reluctant to pay for the necessary improvements.

Elite universities are uniquely able to muster the resources to institute these reforms and thereby improve the quality of undergraduate teaching without arousing determined faculty opposition. As a few universities are already doing, they could gradually replace their part-time adjuncts with full-time instructors hired after a careful search for a renewable terms of years and offered better salaries, benefits, and working conditions. These instructors should be chosen for their ability as teachers and would not be expected to publish. In place of doing traditional research, they would have heavier teaching loads and be encouraged to work with the teaching and learning center to help prepare graduate students as educators and to explore the use of new and improved methods of instruction in their own teaching.*

Skeptics may argue that these instructors will soon find themselves looked down on as second-class faculty by their tenured colleagues and that the new positions will hence be unattractive. The fact is, however, that universities already have a second-class faculty through their extensive use of graduate students, part-time lecturers, and adjunct instructors. The reforms just described will improve their condition in substantial ways that will make such appointments more desirable while simultaneously serving the needs of undergraduate education.

Other professors may fear that in practice, members of the new teaching faculty will be selected and reappointed too casually to avoid the creation of a growing number of aging instructors

---

*One obvious problem with creating a full-time teaching faculty is that it will cost money, since members of the teaching faculty will be paid considerably more than non-tenure-track instructors. This gap is likely to narrow significantly, however, as non-tenure-track instructors join unions and secure substantial pay increases. At the same time, members of the teaching faculty will be paid less and will teach more than tenured professors. Moreover, the necessary changes do not have to come all at once; they can be accomplished gradually, as resources permit. Universities that raise hundreds of millions of dollars per year should be able to create a teaching faculty if they are determined to make this change a priority. I suspect that the real reason for failing to implement the policy has less to do with money than with the fact that no important constituency is clamoring for such a change. If academic leaders make a determined effort to bring about reform and muster the resources to make the changes feasible, they may find the faculty to be persuadable.

who enjoy de facto tenure while no longer bringing new energy and new ideas to improve the teaching of undergraduates. This is a valid concern, but the proper answer must surely be to make special efforts to create a rigorous process of appointment and renewal rather than continue to make do with the flawed system of untenured instructors that exists today.

The replacement of part-time instructors with a full-time teaching faculty will yield a remarkable number of benefits. It will create additional academic positions with considerable job security, higher salaries, and decent working conditions for PhD students who currently face bleak prospects for an academic career. With the help of improved training, these instructors will increase the faculty's capacity for innovation and experimentation in educating undergraduates. Their appointment may help universities fulfill their responsibility for providing instruction in moral reasoning and civic education to all undergraduates. They will also provide able instructors to help prepare graduate (PhD) students to be more competent and knowledgeable educators. Finally, by virtue of their primary focus on improving teaching and learning, they will add a valuable source of insight and knowledge to enrich faculty discussions of undergraduate education.

This last point is important enough to deserve elaboration. In the next decade or two, research universities will need to come to grips with a number of complicated questions about the way they educate students. How should they respond to the growing numbers of older students seeking to increase their knowledge and acquire new skills with maximum convenience and at affordable cost? How will departments answer accreditors who call for more and better evidence of the progress students are making in acquiring desired competencies and knowledge? How will teaching be affected by advances in artificial intelligence and other new technologies? To what extent should colleges try to shift their existing systems of awarding credits from counting the number of hours of completed classroom time to describing the skills and knowledge that students have actually learned so that transcripts reflect what students know and can do rather than merely show how they compare with their classmates?

In addressing such questions, leading universities need to ponder what sort of decision-making body will be best equipped to respond effectively—a faculty entirely composed of experts in specialized fields of knowledge whose time is divided among teaching undergraduates, mentoring doctoral students, and carrying on research, or a faculty that includes some voting members who have been chosen for their promise as teachers, devote most of their time to teaching, and are more familiar than most tenured professors with what is currently known about how students learn and how to measure the progress they are making.

The several initiatives just described may not guarantee the use of new and improved methods of teaching or win immediate agreement from the tenured faculty on other ways to strengthen undergraduate education. But better research can produce stronger evidence of current weaknesses in teaching, while better preparation of PhD candidates and non-tenured instructors should gradually help make faculties more aware of promising new opportunities for increasing student learning.

Improving the Governance of Undergraduate Education

In considering how to improve the methods and content of undergraduate education, academic leaders should do their best to encourage tenured faculty members to continue teaching undergraduates while respecting their need to protect themselves from demands that leave them too little time for their other important responsibilities. In addition, however, it is important that discussions to revise undergraduate education be open to the full range of informed opinion about the needs for reform and the opportunities for improvement. As matters now stand, many individuals with useful ideas and experience, such as members from the staff of teaching and learning centers and student affairs offices, do not participate in any meaningful way in reviews of undergraduate education.* The quality of discussions and the decisions that are reached are likely to suffer as a result.

There is no one way to overcome this problem. The solution will vary in detail according to the particular circumstances of each university. In every case, however, the decision-making process should answer to the same two questions. Do all the groups in the university who possess significant knowledge about undergraduate education have a reasonable opportunity to communicate their ideas to those who ultimately decide on the methods and content of undergraduate education? And do all those who actually play a significant part in teaching undergraduates have an opportunity either to participate or be represented in some fashion in the deliberations and the vote on the eventual outcome?

A FINAL RECKONING

Despite the success of elite universities in attracting huge numbers of undergraduate applicants and graduating almost all who are admitted, significant problems in the quality of undergraduate education remain unsolved and important opportunities for improvement are not being vigorously pursued. Elite universities have unique strengths that could enable them to play an important

---

*For example, during my presidency, William G. Perry Jr., Harvard's director of our Office of Study Counsel (which advised students who encountered difficulty in their courses), wrote a leading book on the development of critical thinking, *Forms of Intellectual and Ethical Development in the College Years: A Scheme* (1970). Nevertheless, he played no role in the faculty's comprehensive review of undergraduate education.

role in finding solutions. If their leaders rise to the occasion and take the initiative in pursuing the possibilities for reform, the next few decades could turn out to be another period of remarkable progress in the quality of education offered by our colleges and universities. With these prospects in mind, presidents of elite universities who are wondering how to make a lasting contribution of genuine importance can find ample opportunities to do so provided they devote the time and effort required for success.

CHAPTER 10

———

The Many Sins of Intercollegiate Athletics

MIDWAY IN MY PRESIDENCY, JUST A DAY AFTER the University of North Carolina basketball team had advanced to the "Final Four" of the national college basketball tournament, its long-serving, highly esteemed president, Bill Friday, called me with an unexpected request: Would I chair a committee of college presidents formed by the American Council on Education to make recommendations for cleaning up the mess of intercollegiate athletics? The committee would be composed of presidents of some of the great athletic powerhouses: Notre Dame, University of Miami, Louisiana State, and the University of Southern California, among others.

Why was I asked to chair such a group? I had imagined that it must be because I was currently serving as board chair of the American Council on Education. Others had a different explanation. According to the president of USC, "We wanted a chair who could be entirely neutral"—a not-so-subtle reference to Harvard's modest stature as an athletic power. Whatever the reason, I soon began a two-year journey into the swamp of intercollegiate sports.

MY FUTILE EFFORT TO REFORM
INTERCOLLEGIATE ATHLETICS

As our committee began its work, the only two member presidents from elite universities failed to show up, either because
they considered the effort to be hopeless or because they found
the subject too embarrassing. The rest of the members, however,
were unusually conscientious in attending the meetings and participating in the discussions. I came to realize that most of them,
like President Friday, were troubled that their university was
engaged in an enterprise in such blatant conflict with traditional
academic values. They had much to be embarrassed about—the
admission of dozens of athletes every year whose academic qualifications were far below those of the rest of the student body;
the creation of special courses and even entire majors that were
designed to be easy enough for even the least academically qualified athletes to complete with little effort; the periodic scandals
over the methods used to recruit highly touted prospects; and the
salaries paid to head coaches of football and basketball that were
typically well above those of their college presidents.

Since the members of my committee saw no way of escaping
from this quagmire by their own individual efforts, they hoped
that together we might discover some feasible rules that would
improve on the existing situation. As we soon found, however,
very little could be accomplished by adopting nationwide rules.
Colleges were simply too different in size, admissions standards,
and resources to allow for uniform requirements. Abolishing
athletic scholarships, for example, would give lower-cost public universities, such as Georgia or Alabama, a big advantage in
recruiting talented student-athletes over the private universities that charged much higher tuitions, such as Northwestern or
Notre Dame. Insisting that colleges require the same average high
school grades and SAT scores in admitting athletes as they do for

choosing other members of the entering class would again give state universities, such as Ohio State or Mississippi, an advantage over much more selective universities, such as Stanford or Duke. Other rules, such as uniform limits on the number of coaches or the size of coaches' salaries, might be hard to administer and would never be enacted since the voting members of the NCAA were mainly coaches and athletic directors.

After much discussion, we decided that the best we could do was to propose two modest rules. The first was to postpone athletic eligibility by a year for any freshman who had received less than a combined score of 700 (out of a possible total score of 1600) on the SAT test or failed to receive at least a 2.0 grade average in twelve units of academic courses (English, math, history, and so on) in high school. Under this rule, entering students whose weak academic credentials put them at risk of flunking out would have a year at college free from the demands of big-time athletic competition in which to establish themselves academically. The requirement to complete a minimum number of serious academic courses in high school in order to be eligible as freshmen would encourage prospective athletes to take classes that would better prepare them for college work. The second rule that we proposed strengthened the requirement that athletes make significant progress toward graduation each year in order to remain eligible for athletics. The aim of this proposal was to increase the graduation rates of athletes, which in many colleges fell below the levels for the student body as a whole.

After intense lobbying of college presidents to persuade them to instruct their representatives at the NCAA convention to support these rules, our proposals passed. Although the new requirements were very modest, however, a small group of colleges objected vociferously to the rule denying freshman eligibility to athletes with combined SAT scores below 700. They had a

BEYOND THE IDEOLOGICAL DIVIDE

point. At several of these colleges, the average SAT score for the entire student body was below 700. In these institutions, student athletes with SAT scores slightly below 700 could hardly be presumed to be academically at risk since their scores would be at least as high as the average for their entire entering class. This controversy underscored the difficulty of finding uniform rules that fitted all the many hundreds of colleges with their widely varied student bodies.

The following year, our committee submitted a bolder proposal. By then, control over the policies of the NCAA had long since drifted completely out of the hands of college presidents. In theory, presidents could attend the NCAA convention and vote on any changes in the rules. In practice, however, few presidents had the time or the desire to attend. The rest were content to leave the task to their athletic directors or coaches. As a result, the rules were actually determined by a body composed of members who were much more interested in the needs of their athletic programs than in upholding the academic standards of their institutions.

To improve on this situation, our committee proposed that all changes to the rules be subject to approval by a mail ballot vote of the presidents. To have our proposal pass, we again conducted a vigorous lobbying effort to have presidents instruct their representatives to vote in favor. I attended the convention to speak, if necessary, for our proposal. Arriving at the meeting, I soon found myself in a decidedly hostile environment. As one representative from a famous athletic powerhouse said to me, "You presidents should keep your noses out of things you don't know anything about."

When our proposal came before the assembled representatives, the chair announced that the vote would be by show of hands. By doing so, the chair made sure that the coaches and athletic directors representing their colleges could vote anonymously and hence feel free to follow their own preferences in disregard of any contrary instructions from their presidents. Predictably, our proposal lost by a large margin.

All in all, while my experience with the committee taught me a lot about the difficulty of using rules to reform intercollegiate athletics, it did little to improve the existing situation. Achieving reform through the actions of individual colleges was equally unlikely. Robert Maynard Hutchins managed to abolish football at the University of Chicago in the 1930s, but even he succeeded only after the team had suffered through many consecutive losing seasons. Such a step would be extremely difficult today, especially for the big-time athletic powers most in need of reform. The opposition of athletes, coaches, outraged alumni, devoted fans in the community, and local sportswriters would be vociferous enough that few presidents would choose to undertake such a move. For many state universities, abandoning a high-profile football or basketball program would actually be impossible because the governor or the legislature would forbid it. Even milder reforms would be difficult for most colleges to install unilaterally because doing so would put them at a disadvantage in competing against the rest of the teams in their conference and other traditional athletic rivals.

Under the constant pressure of competition, the athletic practices in most colleges have gradually deviated more and more from accepted academic norms. In the 1950s, athletes, even in the higher-profile sports, were reasonably representative of the rest of the student body. In fact, athletes in many selective colleges were slightly more likely than nonathletes to graduate in the top third of their class. Those days, however, are long gone. In the few highly selective colleges that belong to major athletic conferences, recruited football and basketball players often have SAT scores as much as 300 points below the average for all admitted students. Well above half of the athletes in high-profile sports at Division I private universities finish in the bottom third of their class.[1]

Recruiting talented athletic prospects has become a much more expensive, high-pressure activity than it was several decades ago. Scandals repeatedly occur over violations of the NCAA's recruiting rules, such as giving under-the-table payments to highly regarded recruits or their families. Meanwhile, the cost of athletic programs continues to rise to ever-higher levels as colleges compete with one another in adding coaches and raising their salaries, increasing recruitment expenditures, and building ever more costly stadiums, all-weather practice fields, weight rooms, and other expensive facilities. Most colleges can ill afford these costs. While a handful of institutions whose teams appear often on television make a handsome profit from their football and basketball teams, the vast majority have to subsidize athletics with increasing amounts of money that could otherwise be spent for academic purposes.

In short, the leading athletic universities that dominate television and attract the most devoted fans have created a juggernaut that they are no longer able to control. The struggle to remain competitive and to compete for success on the athletic field demands relentlessly growing expenditures on state-of-the-art facilities, extensive recruiting, and salary wars to attract the most accomplished coaches. Only a few colleges manage to make a profit from this increasingly costly competition. The rest struggle to survive a process over which they have ceased to have much control.*

---

*According to the sports economist Andrew Zimbalist, only 25 of the 130 top Football Bowl Subdivision (FBS) colleges earned a profit on athletics in 2017. The median annual loss for the remaining schools was $14.5 million. Zimbalist, "Only Congress Can Fix the Lousy Business of College Sports," *Market Watch* (January 26, 2023).

As big-time athletic programs become more commercialized and more time-consuming for the students who participate, public support is growing for treating athletes in revenue-producing sports as professionals who should be paid for their services. In this way, athletes would no longer be exploited by having to spend countless hours of their time with only a free education in return, while their coaches pocket huge salaries paid for by money from television revenues and ticket sales.

A number of states have responded by enacting laws over the objection of the NCAA to allow college athletes to receive money from advertisers who seek their endorsement or simply use the photographs of "star" players to promote their products. These laws have now been upheld by the Supreme Court. It is hard to fathom how intercollegiate athletics will be improved by allowing some members of a team to rake in hundreds of thousands of dollars from commercial deals while other teammates soldier on, unpaid as before. Nor will it help to have alumni businessmen who are devoted fans arranging lucrative endorsement deals to induce especially promising high school athletes to enroll in their alma mater.

Many coaches view the current situation as unsustainable. Nevertheless, now that these laws are on the books and the Supreme Court has upheld them, the next step may be to allow athletes in revenue-producing sports to negotiate with their colleges over salaries. Players in one college have already brought suit to be recognized as employees under the National Labor Relations Act with power to organize and bargain over salaries and other conditions of employment. This step will hardly further the academic values of participating colleges and universities. The leading athletic powers may feel compelled to bargain and pay ever-increasing salaries to their athletes, just as they do for their coaches, in order to remain competitive and preserve their share of television revenues. By doing so, most colleges will lose even more money on athletics, while increasingly resembling the owners of a Minor League Baseball team, surely an incongruous position for a self-respecting university.

Union organizing in big-time athletic powers will do nothing to diminish or eliminate the many compromises that are already being made with basic academic values. Collective bargaining will simply result in a contest over how to distribute the revenues derived from football and basketball and will probably drain more resources from academic activities in order to cover the mounting cost of a successful athletics program. The universities that compete at this level may alter the existing rules to impose some order on the wild scramble that currently exists among colleges to convince the best athletes to enroll. But these reforms will do little to uphold the academic values of the universities involved. Thus, the prospects for reforming big-time athletics seem even more bleak today than they were forty years ago during my unsuccessful effort to bring about improvement.

The outlook seems a bit brighter for the many colleges and universities that do not appear regularly on television or reap anything like the financial rewards available to the big-time athletic powers for their programs. The experience of the Ivies in pursuing this course may therefore throw some light on the possibilities and problems of this approach to athletic reform.

THE IVY LEAGUE REFORMS

Shortly before taking office, I met Bill Bowen, who was then the provost of Princeton. After we shook hands, Bill surprised me by asking whether I would join with him to take a hard look at existing athletic practices in the Ivy League. Although the eight presidents had long since agreed not to give athletic scholarships to

athletes, Bill felt that other practices had arisen that were inconsistent with the academic purposes of the member schools.

Not long thereafter, Bill became president of Princeton and
we began to identify the ways in which competition was eroding
academic values and increasing costs unnecessarily. Our fellow
Ivy presidents were willing partners. Together, we started to look
askance at proposals to increase the number of coaches or to
add more games to lengthen existing schedules. We agreed to
forbid scheduling midweek games that interfered with classes
by requiring athletes to travel outside the immediate area or to
play within a week before final exams, when students needed to
be studying.

After a few years, Bill proposed that we look at the admissions practices of the member schools to see whether the gap
between the SAT scores of athletes and those of other students
had increased over the preceding fifteen years. With the approval
of the member presidents, he set to work to answer this question.
Sure enough, the data showed that the gap for the three high-
profile sports of football, basketball, and ice hockey had gradually
grown bit by bit to become much larger than it had been fifteen
years before. The gap for other sports had also increased, but not
by nearly as much.

Our fellow presidents agreed that something needed to be
done. The discussions that ensued among our deans of admissions resembled an international meeting over arms control as
the negotiators struggled to find a way to maintain parity among
the eight member colleges, which differed significantly in average test scores and numbers of applicants. Eventually, everyone
agreed on a rule that basically required each member to admit
(with very few exceptions) only athletes with SAT scores within
one standard deviation of the median score for the rest of the
class. In this way, admitted athletes might have SAT scores

somewhat below the average, but every athlete would still have scores equal to or above those of many classmates who were not athletes.

Bill and I eventually left office feeling that we had accomplished most of what was needed to protect the academic integrity of the Ivy League schools. That feeling was reinforced one morning during my final year as president when I found to my surprise that Walter Byers, the longtime president of the NCAA and principal architect of its growth and power, had made an appointment to see me. To my even greater surprise, he did not scold me for my earlier efforts to reform the NCAA or boast of his accomplishments as its leader. Instead, he said that he had come to tell me that thinking back over his long career, he had concluded that the Ivy League came the closest to reconciling a robust athletic program with the values appropriate for academic institutions. I believed him at the time. Only later did I come to realize that the problems of Ivy League athletics were more pervasive and more resistant to reform than I had imagined.

Some fifteen years after I retired, when Bowen had become president of the Andrew W. Mellon Foundation, he conducted a study of athletics in a number of highly selective institutions that were not great athletic powers, such as members of the Ivy League and leading small liberal arts colleges in New England.[2] What Bill found was that even in these colleges, the desire to win had gradually given rise to a bumper crop of questionable practices. Since athletic success depended heavily on the ability to enroll the best high school players, the search for better athletes had become an increasingly expensive enterprise, as coaches often searched for talent not only throughout the United States but in other countries around the world. The length and intensity of team practices had also increased as teams introduced off-season conditioning programs and lengthened their seasons in some sports to extend throughout the academic year. More and more games began to be scheduled at times and places that interfered with classroom schedules. As a result, athletes were spending more and more time at their sport, even though their academic records tended to fall below the average for their class. While women's athletics were initially free of the pressures and compromises characteristic of the men's programs, their coaches had gradually begun to adopt many of the practices used by their male counterparts.

The effects of competitive pressures on the academic programs of these selective colleges went well beyond giving athletes an advantage in admissions. Bowen's studies showed that in Ivy League colleges, athletes, especially in football, basketball, and ice hockey, not only performed worse academically than their classmates; they tended to finish with a rank in class that was below what their SAT scores and high school grades had predicted.[3] By Bowen's calculations, though athletes in Ivy League colleges graduated at approximately the same high rates as other students, 81 percent of the recruited male athletes in the high-profile sports and 64 percent of recruited male athletes for the other teams finished with grade averages in the bottom third of their class.[4] For some years, the tendency to underperform existed only for male athletes. By the time of Bowen's study, however, a gap had begun to appear for women athletes and was gradually growing larger.

One might assume that underperformance in the classroom must result from the heavy time demands of competitive athletics. On closer analysis, however, the causes turned out to be more complicated. No persistent underperformance existed among students engaged in other extracurricular activities with heavy time demands. Even more curious was the discovery in the Bowen study that the downward effects of athletics on grades were much more pronounced among recruited athletes than among unrecruited or "walk-on" team members, even though both groups presumably spent the same amount of time in team practice and the weight room. In addition, Bowen found that the effect on grades for recruited athletes in the high-profile sports tended to persist even during off-season semesters when the time demands of athletics were much lower. These findings suggested that there must be something about being a *recruited* athlete that had a particularly pronounced effect on academic performance.[5]

UNFINISHED BUSINESS

Bowen's study, published fifteen years after he had retired from Princeton, made clear that the Ivy League reforms that we initiated had not done away with all the problems of intercollegiate athletics. At least three important issues were still unresolved. One was the increasing emphasis on recruiting and the growing percentage of students in each incoming class who were recruited and admitted for their athletic ability. The second persistent problem was procedural. Members of a league could accomplish a lot by agreeing on safeguards and other limits among themselves. But how could they make sure that these agreements would withstand the constant pressure by coaches to find new ways to gain a competitive edge over their opponents? Finally, might individual colleges diminish the growing costs and other problems of athletics by simply dropping certain sports from intercollegiate competition or reducing them to club sports with many fewer coaches and no recruiting or preferential admission of athletes?

Feasible Reforms

Bowen's study of Ivy League members and liberal arts colleges called attention to the high percentages of each entering class that were made up of recruited athletes. Because the student bodies of the colleges he studied were comparatively small and the number of competitive sports had increased, the cohort of student athletes admitted to liberal arts colleges on the recommendation of coaches had grown to make up as much as 20 percent or more of the entire entering class. Elite universities admitted more students, but athletes still amounted to a sizable fraction of the student body. The addition of women's teams added many more athletes to each entering class. As a result, the athletic programs of elite colleges had now drifted further from their basic aim of admitting students with the highest potential for making significant contributions to society.

This conflict cannot be eradicated completely. Coaches must have some way of making sure that they will have enough pitchers, linemen, and point guards to field competitive teams. But presidents could at least agree on restrictions to minimize the damage to their academic priorities. They could impose lower limits on the number of athletes who can be recruited for each sport. They could tighten the academic requirements for admitting recruited athletes to bring their high school grades and SAT scores to levels closer to those of the rest of the student body. They could forbid their teams from competing in tournaments for national championships, since the chance of gaining an invitation to these events and making a strong showing is a major incentive for doing whatever it takes to compete at a high level. Coaches may protest these reforms, arguing that their teams will have a hard time playing against schools outside their league, but the appropriate remedy for this problem is surely to schedule different colleges rather than lower the admissions requirements for athletes.

These steps would not eradicate the problems associated with recruited athletes identified in the Bowen study, still less do away with all the other compromises associated with American intercollegiate athletics. Some seemingly useful remedies, such as reducing the number of hours per day for athletes to practice, are simply too hard to enforce. Nevertheless, feasible reforms exist that would go a long way toward limiting the damage to academic values.*

Overseeing Athletic Programs

It is one thing to introduce rules and another to enforce them carefully enough to keep them from gradually eroding. The experience of the Ivy League reveals how difficult it is to provide effective oversight. Without it, however, coaches will eventually find

---

*It should be noted that the power of conferences such as the Ivy League to improve their current athletic practices could be severely limited by the courts if the plaintiffs prevail in a lawsuit recently brought by Brown University athletes. The plaintiffs in this case argue that the agreement among Ivy League schools not to offer athletic scholarships amounts to illegal price fixing under the Sherman Antitrust Act.

A ruling in the athletes' favor would be extremely unfortunate and quite undeserved. The agreement of the Ivies, unlike unlawful price-fixing schemes, is not designed to maximize profits. Ivies regularly lose large sums from their athletic programs. The purpose of their agreement is to treat all their students the same depending only on their ability to pay and to encourage athletes to enroll because of the quality of the education they will receive and not because they have been offered the most money.

Only through agreements among the members of a league can universities resist the pressure of competition from forcing them to compromise admissions standards, course requirements, and other academic values in the constant struggle to avoid being disadvantaged on the athletic field. Requiring Ivy League schools to pay their athletes and viewing their agreements as conspiracies in restraint of trade would thus give rise to all the ills besetting big-time athletic programs. Rather than open the door to commercializing Ivy League athletics, judges should affirm the Ivies' long-standing agreement by invoking the "rule of reason" established over a century ago in construing the application of the Sherman Act. For a contrary view, see Aaron Solomon, "Ivy League Schools Are Not Above Compensating Their Student-Athletes Fairly," *Fortune*, April 14, 2023.

new ways that conflict with academic values in order to prevail on the athletic field. The problem is not that coaches are irresponsible. Those whom I have known have almost all been fine and honorable human beings. But coaches cannot help having a keen desire to win. In a league, if any one coach finds a way to gain an advantage, the other coaches have no choice but to do the same.

Effective oversight is hard to achieve because the desire for athletic success is continuous, the erosion of academic values is often hard to detect, and not all presidents may share the zeal required to preserve strict limits. Thus, the slow but steady growth in the gap between the SAT scores of Ivy League athletes and the rest of their classmates went unnoticed by the member presidents for fifteen years (and probably longer), until President Bowen insisted on a careful longitudinal study of admissions data. The subsequent discovery that recruited athletes perform less well in the classroom than their walk-on teammates was an unexpected result that could not be detected by simply looking at the usual facts and figures supplied each year to Ivy League presidents for their review. Thus, the Ivy experience suggests a need for more exacting oversight of athletics coupled with a capability independent of the athletic program to initiate and carry out rigorous studies, not only of the financial costs of intercollegiate sports but of the effects of the athletic program on the academic values shared by member colleges.

Reducing the Number of Teams

Since the Ivy League and most other highly selective colleges do not earn nearly enough from television appearances and ticket sales to offset their rising athletic costs, more and more money must be diverted from academic programs to fund their sports programs. There is one final way, however, by which colleges can limit and even reduce the financial and academic costs of intercollegiate athletics. They can cut the number of teams they field. Unlike the two measures just discussed, eliminating teams does not require agreement among all members of the conference. For example, Brown University did not have to get permission from other Ivy League colleges when it announced in 2020 that it was permanently canceling several team sports in an effort to save money.

Canceling a sport is never easy, but some teams are much easier to discontinue than others. Abandoning football by an Ivy League college would almost certainly result in loud protests not only from players and other students, but from alumni, local sportswriters, and others. Even less prominent teams may be difficult for some colleges to drop. Stanford University announced after COVID-19 struck that it was discontinuing eleven teams in an effort to offset the financial losses caused by the pandemic. Eventually, however, Stanford had to rescind these cuts after several thousand alumni signed a petition protesting such action, demonstrations took place, and students brought suit charging a violation of Title IX of the Civil Rights Act, which guarantees equal opportunities for male and female athletes.

Resistance as intense as the opposition Stanford encountered, however, may not be typical. In all, several hundred teams were successfully dropped by colleges during the pandemic. If economic conditions such as a recession force colleges to cut expenses, there is no compelling reason why canceling a few sports or reconstituting them as club sports cannot be successfully included among a series of other budget cuts. The real issue is whether there is a sufficiently convincing argument for making what many people may consider a cruel and unnecessary decision.

The case for reducing the number of teams or reconstituting them as club sports is stronger than most people appreciate.

Although there are a host of valuable and popular extracurricular activities such as student orchestras and theater groups, community service programs, debating clubs, and political organizations, none approaches intercollegiate athletics in the amount of coaching and adult supervision they receive, the elaborate facilities they require, the travel they entail, and much else. None of them requires the compromises routinely made with academic admissions standards in order to enroll appropriately talented student participants. None has been shown to result in the systemic academic underperformance that is so characteristic among recruited athletes. Even if one lumped together all the other extracurricular activities, the subsidies they receive and the compromises made to enroll sufficient numbers of highly skilled participants would not begin to approach the costs and compromises of intercollegiate athletics. Meanwhile, important academic needs remain underfunded, such as the meager salaries and benefits paid to non-tenure-track instructors, the insufficient support for research to improve undergraduate education, and the lack of an adequate program for training PhD students as teachers, not merely as researchers.

Proposals to drop existing teams, however, will typically give rise to much magical thinking from opponents about the benefits of intercollegiate athletics. Supporters often claim that athletics build school spirit even though this is true at best for only a few of the dozens of sports supported by many universities and ignores existing evidence that most alumni from selective colleges believe that athletics are emphasized *too much* by their alma mater.[6] Others will claim that athletics build character despite the lack of any supporting evidence and despite the tendency for athletes to be amply represented among the perpetrators of sexual assaults on campus and the participants in the occasional incidents of mass student cheating on exams. Still other fans will claim that athletes are more likely to become leaders in later life as well as generous donors to their university, even though careful studies have failed to find convincing evidence to support either assertion.[7]

The strongest argument for intercollegiate athletics is that participants gain enormous satisfaction from their sport and from the friendships they enjoy with their teammates. There is undoubtedly some truth to this argument. Having read many reflective essays by graduating Harvard athletes, I can testify to the countless expressions of gratitude to coaches and appreciation for the bonds forged with other members of their teams.

Even so, I remain unconvinced that these satisfactions outweigh the costs and compromises associated with college sports. I recognize the intense pleasure students derive from playing on university teams, but I have yet to encounter any evidence that athletes are more satisfied with their college experience than other members of their class. I also suspect that the satisfaction gained from belonging to a team is acquired at some cost to the benefits that athletes might receive if they had time to participate more widely in the activities of the university and explore the diversity of its student body. Besides, at least some of the enjoyment students derive from athletics could be preserved for many sports by reconstituting teams as club sports with far less coaching, travel, and other costs associated with intercollegiate competition today.

In the end, therefore, the enjoyment of participants in intercollegiate athletics comes at a high price. In a time when there are not enough places in elite colleges to accommodate every applicant with exceptional potential to contribute to society, it is hard to justify setting aside such a large fraction of the entering class in order to compete effectively on the playing field. When leading colleges cannot pay a decent salary to the non-tenure-track instructors who do an increasing share of undergraduate teaching, it is likewise difficult to justify the expense of providing the multiple coaches, extensive travel, and state-of-the-art facilities that are needed to field twenty, thirty, or more teams engaged in intercollegiate competition.

PROSPECTS FOR REFORM

In light of all the problems associated with intercollegiate athletics, what is the likelihood that elite colleges will introduce substantial, lasting reform? As noted previously, the chances for agreeing on major improvements in colleges that play at the highest level seem extremely small. Among the elite institutions that compete at this level, most are state universities that have a host of avid fans among the public, politicians, alumni, and even their trustees. The opposition to truly substantial reform would simply be too great to be overcome. At most, one or two of the few private elites that belong to a big-time "power" conference may someday abandon high-profile competition and try to join a league with more modest ambitions.

The prospects for reform are considerably brighter for the leading colleges that do not compete at the highest level. The feasibility of curbing the worst excesses of intercollegiate athletics has already been demonstrated by a number of first-rate universities such as Chicago, Washington in St. Louis, MIT, and others that compete among themselves with much lower athletic budgets and fewer serious compromises with academic values.

Keeping existing low-key athletics programs from gradually relaxing their standards is much easier than eliminating teams altogether, dialing back recruiting, and taking the other steps that are needed to reform a more robust athletic program. A transformation of the latter kind will inflict considerable pain and provoke much resistance from the athletes and coaches whose lives will be affected by the reforms. Although many students and alumni appear to favor a lower-key athletic program in principle, they are unlikely to lend much active support for reforms when they are proposed.

Under these conditions, presidents may be unwilling to initiate the changes needed to make athletic programs truly compatible with academic values despite the persuasive arguments for doing so. Presidents have enough difficult problems to solve without agreeing to create new ones. Moreover, most presidents want their students to have a thoroughly enjoyable and satisfying college experience. Initiating reforms that will cause immediate disappointment for a significant group of students is a peculiarly distasteful step for a president to take.

Less drastic reforms, however, such as cutting recruitment budgets, making athletic schedules more compatible with academic responsibilities, raising academic requirements for admitting athletes, and even reducing the number of athletes receiving athletic preferences for admission are all within the realm of possibility. As a result, presidents of most elite universities can still take significant steps to bring their athletic programs into closer conformity with academic values even if they cannot bring themselves to reduce the number of teams they currently field for intercollegiate competition.

CHAPTER 11

———

Dire Thoughts before Daybreak about
the Future of Elite Universities

MORE THAN THIRTY YEARS HAVE PASSED SINCE
I resigned as president in 1991, and fifteen years have
come and gone since I returned unexpectedly for an
additional year of service while Harvard searched for a new president. Nevertheless, since old habits die slowly, I still lie awake
occasionally in the wee hours of the morning and worry about
the future of even our strongest and most distinguished universities. My concerns have nothing to do with whether Harvard will
be eclipsed by Stanford or some other enterprising institution.
Nor do I find myself agitated over the threat of an unexpected
catastrophe, such as the coronavirus pandemic or another severe
recession. Rather, what worries me most are three slow-growing
problems with no evident solution that could eventually limit
the capacity of universities such as Harvard to make their most
important contributions to students and society.

THE FULLY ORGANIZED UNIVERSITY

As the year 2020 neared its end, some four thousand undergraduates at Columbia took the unusual step of threatening to withhold

their second-semester tuitions to protest the amount the administration was charging them. In addition, they demanded a seat at the table when the university considered issues that directly affected the lives of students. This was not the first collective action by students dissatisfied with the amounts they were charged during the pandemic for a remote version of college they considered much inferior. Undergraduates at the University of Chicago had previously threatened a "tuition strike" and were said to have received some concessions from the administration before finally sending off their checks.

In 2022, 48,000 postdoctoral fellows, research assistants, and PhD students serving as teaching assistants went on strike at all of the University of California's campuses, claiming that the salaries they received were too meager to pay for their most basic living expenses. The strike lasted for almost six weeks, during which many classes were canceled. By the time the strike ended, protestors had disrupted a meeting of the Board of Regents, invaded the corporate offices of a prominent member of the board, blocked the hallway outside the office of the Berkeley chancellor, picketed her home, and occupied various university buildings. In the end, though the strikers did not win everything they asked for, they did gain pay increases averaging close to 50 percent over two years, along with a variety of other benefits and reforms.

These efforts are only the latest chapters in a long and gradual increase in collective action that has spread throughout American universities. The building trades began the process during the 1930s and 1940s. Since then, one segment after another of the university population has organized itself to negotiate with the administration. The most recent additions have been research assistants and graduate (PhD) students, such as those involved in the University of California strike, who have now won elections under the National Labor Relations Act at a number of research universities.

Most undergraduates have a different legal status since they can hardly be classified as employees qualified to affiliate with a traditional union and acquire the right to compel their universities to bargain with them under the National Labor Relations Act. Even so, if enough undergraduates band together to withhold their tuition, they may have the power to demand the right to negotiate. Student athletes in one university have brought suit claiming the right to be classified as employees and to bargain over wages and working conditions.

This gradual increase in collective action raises several questions. Is the fully organized university a welcome prospect? What does it portend for the governance of universities? What will be its benefits and costs?

During my presidency, union officials made a determined effort to organize Harvard's clerical and technical employees. The campaign went on for years but eventually led to an election late in my term of office in which the union prevailed by some fifty votes in an employee unit of well over one thousand members. Drafting a contract from scratch for such a large and diverse group of employees promised to be a formidable task, but I was able to enlist the help of two remarkably experienced faculty friends from my years of teaching labor law. One was John Dunlop, former Secretary of Labor, with decades of experience solving labor disputes. The other was Jim Healy, a Harvard Business School professor whose long career in labor relations included being chosen by the Ford Motor Company and the United Auto Workers to arbitrate employee grievances that proved to be impossible to settle. Both men were held in high regard by the union leadership. With their assistance, we managed to negotiate a contract that was costly but satisfactory to both sides.

When I returned to the presidency more than fifteen years later, I concluded that even though unionization was initially expensive, the results had improved the University. Subsequent negotiations had been completed successfully with no disruptions. Benefits were bargained for that improved the quality of life for many employees. Fortunately, we had the benefit of an unusual labor leader, Kris Rondeau. As we were starting out just after the election, Kris volunteered to me her belief about her role. "I would regard a strike as a huge personal failure," she remarked. "My goal is to make each contract a win for Harvard as well as a win for our employees." So far as I could tell years later, she had lived up to that standard.

It does not automatically follow from this one experience that a fully organized university with negotiators bargaining for every segment of its workforce and student body will be an unqualified improvement over the hierarchical system that universities enjoyed during much of their history. There are respectable arguments on both sides of this question. Some will argue that all constituencies have a legitimate stake in the way the university operates, so all should have a seat at the table in considering policies that will affect the members of their group. On the other hand, many university leaders will shudder at the thought of having to bargain separately with such a long list of organized groups over budgets and other issues. They will fear that some union leaders will not fully appreciate all the stakes involved in these negotiations, including the interests of future students and employees. Most of all, they will worry that the university will suffer from recurrent disruptions as more and more groups gain the power to take collective actions that interfere with the operation of the institution and the lives of other members of the university community.

Both sides to this issue have legitimate arguments. I would reluctantly agree that segments in the university that do not have an organized voice often find their interests neglected. Even the best-intentioned campus leaders have a tendency to slight the unorganized when hard budgetary choices must be made. For example, when our technical and clerical workers still had no union, I believed that Harvard paid these employees as much as any employer in the Boston area. Our managers had told me so. On careful review, however, we discovered that my impression was incorrect. Although our current pay was above the average for the area, we had allowed it to slip below the level at several leading Boston-area employers during the stagflation that had stretched the University's finances during the 1970s and early 1980s. Similar examples throughout the nation's colleges and universities are not hard to find. The low pay and shabby working conditions of tens of thousands of part-time adjunct instructors provide an obvious case in point. Women who are victims of sexual abuse have been discouraged from pursuing their complaints in order to protect the university from adverse publicity. Graduate (PhD) students whose future careers depend on the support of their thesis advisers have often had no recourse when they have suffered from unfair treatment from a domineering mentor.

At the same time, campus officials have good reason to feel apprehensive as the trend toward organization continues. When more and more units organize, the time required to negotiate with twenty or more different groups increases, along with the likelihood that innocent third parties will suffer from strikes or other collective actions by disgruntled unions. Students have become experts in using adverse publicity and the threat of disruption to strengthen their demand that presidents and other academic officers pay immediate attention to their concerns. They are often unmoved by the long-term consequences of their demands, claiming that a university with a multibillion-dollar endowment can easily afford to do more. University officials, on the other hand, realize that most of the endowment is legally restricted to the purposes prescribed by the donors and worry (sometimes excessively) that using endowment principal to pay for union proposals can become a habit that will sacrifice the future welfare of the institution and its members in order to satisfy the current desires of students and employees.

The costs of disagreement can be substantial. At Yale, for example, relations with its largest union were embittered and disruptive for decades. During one prolonged strike, classes could no longer be conducted on campus, and more and more professors became disgruntled. Eventually, a number of faculty members published a scathing critique of the president's response to the union in the campus newspaper. He resigned not long thereafter. As he told me at the time, "I was so disheartened by the action of my colleagues that I could hardly force myself to get up in the morning and come to work."

Intractable differences of opinion periodically arise in a university that no amount of negotiation can resolve. The disagreement with Columbia students over the appropriate tuition during the coronavirus pandemic offers an apt example. The students insisted that they should not have to pay the normal increase in tuition for a form of education that obviously fell short of the "full" college experience. One can certainly understand and sympathize with their position. University officials, however, responded that they were experiencing substantial losses because of the pandemic owing to the added cost of adapting to fully online instruction and the loss of income for room and board when all or most students could not live on campus. Since the full per-student cost of education at Columbia already exceeded the tuition by a substantial margin, students were still getting a bargain, thanks to the endowment, even if they had to pay a bit more. Besides, in exchange for paying the increased tuition, students learning online were continuing to advance at the normal pace toward graduating, earning their diploma, and receiving the economic benefits of an elite college degree.

There is no way of settling a dispute of this kind by logic or evidence alone. Cool heads will not always prevail. The controversy may eventually have to be resolved in favor of the side most willing to absorb the losses resulting from the tuition strike.

There are steps the government can take to reduce the likelihood of needless or irresponsible disruptions in the fully organized university. Laws could be passed that require the opposing parties to accept the appointment of a trained mediator or that mandate a cooling-off period before resorting to a strike. Such measures can help but often do not. In the end, therefore, the gradual organization of every group on campus remains a problem without a fully satisfactory solution.

THE QUEST FOR MONEY

Most of the activities and aspirations of elite universities share one feature in common. They all cost money. The constant effort to pursue new opportunities and meet new needs requires the funds to hire more professors, add to the staff, and provide better facilities. The tendency of most universities to start new programs rather than close unsuccessful ones is expensive. The pressure to enroll more minority and low-income students requires hefty increases in financial aid.

The never-ending needs of this kind have led to a steadily growing effort to raise more money and build a larger and larger "development" program, as the process has come to be described. The growth is gradual, but its effects over time are enormous. When I took office in 1971, there were only two full-time fund-raising specialists shared by the central administration with the Faculty of Arts and Sciences, along with perhaps eight or ten additional professionals scattered throughout the rest of the University. When I returned for a year in 2006 as interim president, I learned that it was now customary to speak to the fund-raisers and alumni affairs officers at the beginning of each academic year. My talk took place in the University theater before an audience of several hundred people seated and many more who had to stand in the back. I remember thinking as I walked to the podium that if I were recalled to duty again in another fifteen to twenty years, the meeting would probably have to take place in the Harvard football stadium.

The growth of the development staff cannot be dismissed as just another example of needless administrative bloat. During the first year of my presidency, Harvard raised a total of only $41 million, and that was considered normal. Only a few years earlier, my predecessor had successfully completed the largest fund drive ever attempted by a university by raising slightly more than $80 million over a five-year period. Today, however, Harvard raises more than $1 *billion* every year. Such huge amounts obviously require a far larger and more professional staff than I or my predecessors could have possibly imagined. Even so, the benefits gained far outweigh the added administrative costs.

Despite the impressive results and the improvements they have made possible, I worry about the side effects of these gigantic efforts—not just for Harvard but for all the leading institutions, including the flagship public universities that have had to resort to full-scale fund-raising to offset the gradual disinvestment by their state government. Some of the most obvious effects involve the president. Fund-raising demands a large and growing share of a leader's time. Asking wealthy prospects for gifts is only a small part of the task. Speaking to alumni gatherings both in America and increasingly in countries throughout the world is also essential to the effort. Capital fund drives, including the preliminary planning and talks with select groups of potential donors even before the drive begins, are now important items on every president's agenda. Since these drives occur with increasing frequency, the efforts they require consume a large and growing portion of a leader's term in office, while the time available to deal with academic affairs necessarily shrinks.

Slowly but surely, the quest for funds also plays a part in more and more activities on elite campuses. Class reunions are one example: each reunioning class is encouraged to vie with others to raise the largest reunion gift. Parents weekends become an opportunity to talk with wealthy fathers and mothers about the opportunities to contribute to the quality of their child's educa-tion. At many universities, football games have become a valuable tool for persuading prospective donors to come to the campus and sit with the president in special seats or expensive luxury boxes reserved for the purpose. Groups of successful alumni have been formed on some campuses, ostensibly to gain their expertise for advising campus leaders on a variety of problems but, more important, to arouse their interest in contributing money to their alma mater.

The need to raise more money has also become a threat to basic values. In universities with high-profile athletic teams, the need to compete successfully and gain an increasing share of tele-vision revenues leads to a gradual erosion of academic standards. On many campuses, fund-raising has corrupted the admissions process by giving preferences to the children of existing and prospective donors. The hope of added revenue has lured some universities into commercial ventures, such as acquiring stock in start-up companies founded by their professors, which can lose money and create undesirable conflicts of interest.

Fund-raising has also affected appointments to key univer-sity positions. No presidential search committee today could say with a straight face what members of the Harvard Corporation said to me in 1970 when I told them that I was not a suitable candidate for the presidency because I hated to raise money: "If Harvard is well-managed," one Corporation member replied, "the fund-raising will take care of itself." That remark may have been innocently made, but it was not true then and is far less true today. It is likely that some universities will fail to appoint the most accomplished candidates for president because some other candidate appears to have greater promise for raising money. In other universities, worthy candidates for college presidencies may decline to serve because they simply do not wish to spend so much of their time asking for money. These risks are likely to increase as fund-raising goals grow ever higher.

As the sums that need to be raised each year continue to rise, more and more faculty members must be enlisted to participate in the effort. Provosts and deans now join in the task. Heads of research centers, departments, and teaching programs are often expected to help out, presumably at some cost to their research, teaching, and other academic pursuits. Professors are frequently asked to cover a large part of their salaries by getting grants for their research.

Fund-raising also enters into the selection of persons to fill important volunteer positions at universities. Trustees are often chosen primarily or in part for their ability to make large gifts. In some universities, boards have been expanded in size to make room for more potential donors. As this process continues, board meetings may spend less time on real problems and increasingly come to resemble dog and pony shows designed to impress the trustees and acquaint them with all the great things the university is doing.

Still other costs are more subtle. As presidents spend more and more of their time talking in glowing terms about their universities to prospective donors, they may come to believe what they are saying and begin to minimize the gravity of problems on their campuses or even deny their existence altogether. The excessive optimism of many presidents regarding the job readiness of their graduates, a view disputed by most employers, provides a telling illustration.[1]

The importance of raising funds also contributes to a growing temptation to avoid negative publicity in order to protect the reputation of the university. For a long time, universities did not disclose the number of crimes on their campuses until the government insisted that they be published. Acts of sexual abuse in several universities have been suppressed or ignored for years, only to be exposed eventually at great cost to the institution. The repeated abuse of children over many years by an assistant football coach at Penn State University even led to the trial and temporary conviction of the president. The sexual improprieties of a well-known gynecologist over many years at the University of Southern California resulted in an eventual settlement with the victims costing the university approximately $1 billion.

Having observed the pervasive effects of fund-raising on the behavior of universities and the duties of their presidents, I regard the incessant search for gifts as a significant problem. Once again, however, I am unable to perceive a solution. Universities will continue to need more and more money to operate successfully. New possibilities for useful activity will undoubtedly emerge that require additional funds. These demands must be met if universities are to exploit opportunities for valuable research, satisfy the creative ambitions of their ablest faculty members, and meet the evolving needs of the society. Government grants will pay for some of the added expense, but not for all of it all of the time. Tuitions may rise to keep up with inflation, but tuitions are already so high that it seems unrealistic to expect them to do much more than that.

In short, it is hard to envision a future for elite universities that does not include a large and growing need to raise money to support the creative energy of these institutions and avoid stagnation and eventual decline. Like the increasing unionization of every segment of the university, the constant search for funds with all its accompanying difficulties seems destined to continue growing with no end in sight. Government grants may help, but such assistance cannot be counted on and tends to bring other disadvantages that give rise to my next and last nocturnal worry.

GOVERNMENT REGULATION

In 1957 Justice Felix Frankfurter, a former professor at the Harvard Law School, wrote the majority opinion for the Supreme Court in *Sweezy v. New Hampshire*.[2] In it he included a sweeping summary of the limited role that government should play in university affairs. He first defined "the four essential freedoms of a university—to determine for itself on academic grounds who may teach, what may be taught, how it should be taught, and who shall be admitted to study." While acknowledging that these activities could not be completely free from government regulation, he declared that "for society's good, political power must abstain from intrusion into this activity of freedom except for reasons that are exigent and compelling."

Frankfurter's opinion has not fared well with the passage of time. Since his words appeared, U.S. presidents, governors, legislators, judges, and civil servants have all stretched the meaning of "exigent and compelling" to uphold a growing number of rules and requirements that erode the "essential freedoms" enumerated by the justice. Beginning in 1978, the Supreme Court began to narrow the freedom of universities to consider race in admitting students. Several states enacted laws ordering public universities to require their students to take a course on American history. A few states even approved legislation requiring professors in public universities to teach a minimum number of hours per week. But interventions of this kind were rare and, in the case of required amounts of teaching, seldom enforced. Until the present century, government officials continued to give substantial autonomy to universities to decide whom to hire for the faculty and how professors should do their work.

In the past decade, however, the role of government regulation has taken a new and more dangerous turn. Increasingly, state and federal officials have begun to intervene in matters of educational policy and to overrule the decisions of colleges and universities on such academic questions as selecting which scholars and scientists to appoint, when they may be terminated, and how they should teach their classes.

Several states have defunded programs that teach students about race using an approach often referred to as "critical race theory." In Ohio, a proposed state law not only would require all college students to take a course on American history but would stipulate the material that students in such courses must read and discuss. Several state governments have refused to fund administrative staffs to promote diversity, equity, and inclusion and assumed responsibility themselves for deciding how their public universities should go about encouraging civil and respectful discourse on their campuses. Several states have taken steps to weaken the practice of tenure. In Florida, Governor DeSantis has even appointed new trustees and replaced the president of one state college with the avowed intention of choosing new professors and transforming it into a conservative institution.*

This shift in the exercise of power over academic policies from faculties and their deans and presidents to state officials and their chosen appointees poses serious threats to the quality of higher education. Government officials and university trustees will normally be less qualified than faculty members to decide such questions as who should be appointed as professors and deans, what courses should be offered, and how controversial subjects should be taught. Moreover, mistaken decisions by government officials are likely to have more serious effects than errors of judgment by professors and deans. When a single university errs, the consequences are felt only by its students, faculty, and employees. When state or federal officials impose a misguided policy, the harm is typically far greater because the government's rules apply to large numbers of institutions. A system of higher education operating under extensive government rules and regulation is also likely to be less innovative and less responsive to the varying needs and desires of a large student population than a system made up of many separate institutions that are largely free to make their own academic decisions.† That is probably why so many leading universities of the world are private institutions that operate with little government control over their academic decision making.

*DeSantis has declared war against "woke" instruction. His lawyer defines "woke" as "the belief that there are systemic injustices in American society and the need to address them." Jonathan Feingold, "Florida Gov. Ron DeSantis Leads GOP Charge against Racial and Gender Equity ahead of 2024," *Newsone,* January 21, 2023. At this point it is not clear how much of DeSantis's campaign will survive judicial scrutiny.

†In fairness, a national system of higher education that has less government regulation may also be more likely to have a substantial number of colleges and universities of very poor quality.

There are difficulties associated with political interventions in academic affairs that are especially serious in a highly polarized political environment such as that of the United States today. As control moves from Democrats to Republicans or vice versa, government policies toward higher education will shift accordingly, causing sudden policy changes that will disrupt the orderly conduct of academic affairs. These tendencies are particularly strong during times like the present when politics have become especially partisan and divisive. It is no accident, then, that Republican legislatures have recently begun to intervene in matters traditionally left for educators to decide in an effort to shift the academic policies of their public universities to reflect more conservative values by dismantling offices of diversity, equity, and inclusion, weakening the protections of tenure, and defunding courses that teach critical race theory.

Because of these recent developments, the growth of government regulation has come to pose a serious threat to the quality of higher education. Even so, no one can deny the essential role that public officials have long played and must continue to play in the affairs of colleges and universities. Governments remain indispensable both for providing essential financial support and for issuing regulations to prevent obviously unfair and improper behavior. As a result, like the other trends discussed in this chapter, the role of government promises to be another problem that seems destined to become increasingly serious, with no effective solution in sight.

THE FUTURE THAT AWAITS ACADEMIC LEADERS

As I contemplate the issues examined in this chapter, I worry about the future for our universities and especially for their leaders. More and more of their time will be consumed by the necessity of responding to the demands of organized constituencies, raising ever-increasing amounts of money, fending off threatening government interventions, and coping with new laws and regulations. Although these duties are essential, they divert more and more of a president's efforts from the most important tasks of the university—educating students and producing the highest quality of research.

These trends also threaten to make the job of leading a university less attractive by forcing presidents to delegate more and more authority over academic affairs to deans and chief academic officers. Bureaucracy will grow with its irritating, time-consuming procedures for arriving at decisions. Presidents will remain in office for shorter periods, and promising candidates may no longer be willing to serve. As responsibility for teaching and learning is shifted to subordinate officials, it will be increasingly necessary for universities to improve their current methods for identifying and evaluating prospective candidates for all levels of academic administration.

Even if universities do a better job of developing capable mid-level academic leaders, however, vital tasks will remain that only presidents, provosts, and deans have the stature and authority to carry out. Only they can select key subordinates, choose which academic programs most need strengthening, and decide which new initiatives deserve the time and resources that ultimate success will require. If excellent candidates for these leadership positions cannot be found within the existing faculty, the university is bound to suffer. While able people to fill these positions can sometimes be recruited from elsewhere, there are added risks in hiring candidates for important positions from outside the institution. As a result, consistently strong leadership will again require better and more systematic methods for identifying, developing, and choosing candidates from within the institution and helping them acquire the necessary knowledge to carry out their academic responsibilities successfully.

Will university presidents and their provosts and deans be able to find enough time to build stronger programs of teaching and research while also attending to the growing administrative demands discussed in this chapter? Will the wisest and most thoughtful faculty members still wish to accept top administrative positions as the work involved becomes more burdensome and less agreeable? And even if sufficiently skillful academic leaders exist, will government officials and politicians intervene in additional ways that undermine the best efforts of presidents and their faculties to strengthen and improve their universities? It is at this point that daybreak comes and my mind can return to simpler problems such as making breakfast, a task that I assumed for the family more than sixty years ago and never managed to relinquish, even during my years as president.

Once I awaken and my sober self returns, I take solace from the fact that analysts have repeatedly forecast a dire future for higher education only to be proved wrong. Conceivably, fate will intervene once again. Perhaps the federal government will provide fresh infusions of money, or perhaps new developments in technology will lower costs, improve learning, and produce added sources of revenue. Whatever happens, many universities are still blessed with well-intentioned leaders, gifted professors, caring trustees, and generous donors. Together, they may somehow find a way of coping with the looming problems while capitalizing on the emerging opportunities. As the saying goes, "It is always darkest before dawn."

———

What Elite Universities Could Do

TODAY, ELITE UNIVERSITIES FIND THEMSELVES IN A curious predicament. By most outward appearances, they are flourishing. And yet, notwithstanding their success, they are continually subjected to harsh criticism from both sides of America's ideological divide. Liberals argue that they are not doing enough to diversify their student bodies and insist that they use their reputations and their endowments to resist activities by corporations that contribute to suffering and injustice in the world. Conservatives distrust them because so many of their professors are liberals and are suspected of influencing the political and racial attitudes of their students.*

*Exaggerated and misleading commentary about elite universities is not always aimed at promoting liberal or conservative policies. Two recent essays criticizing leading universities featured in the *New York Times* illustrate the point. In one piece titled "Elite Universities Are Out of Touch: Blame the Campus" (August 2, 2022), Nick Burns argues that students in elite universities do not understand the real world because they isolate themselves in fortress-like campuses. The author offers no proof that elite professors and students *are* "out of touch," nor does he take any account of the highly diverse backgrounds of student bodies in today's elite universities or the many hundreds of students who are engaged each year in community service programs working in urban schools,

CONCLUSION

THE CRITICISMS

Most of the liberal complaints are expressed by faculty members or students from elite universities. Their criticisms are accurate in identifying a number of questionable admissions policies by elites. But many authors who criticize the failure of elites to admit more low-income students pay little heed to all that these universities are currently doing and ignore the practical difficulties of doing a great deal more. Many of the remedies liberals suggest, such as choosing students by lottery or trying to limit pollution by divesting the stock of fossil fuel companies, would not solve the problems they are meant to overcome and could put at risk important values of academic institutions. Still other liberal proposals, such as building new satellite campuses to educate more lower-income students, would be extremely expensive without giving these applicants the added career advantages of graduating from an elite university.

Conservative critiques are broader in scope and frequently arrive at sweeping conclusions with little or no supporting data. As Victor D. Hanson from the Hoover Institution recently declared in the *New York Post*: "Eventually, even elite schools will lose their current veneer of prestige. Their costly cattle brands will

housing projects, prisons, and homeless shelters. On October 8, 2022, Jessica Calarco authored another essay on the opinion page of the *New York Times* titled "A Professor's Firing Reveals a Lot about Elite Colleges." Professor Calarco takes elite colleges to task for not offering enough assistance to help students such as a young woman with little money "who has to work 20 hours a week to pay bills, doesn't have a reliable laptop or Wi-Fi at her apartment so she has to do her work in a computer lab or on her phone." What the author does not recognize is that low-income students at most elite colleges do not have to work twenty hours per week because they receive enough financial aid to graduate without owing money or having to work during term time. They typically have rooms in university residence halls without needing to pay rent or go to a computer lab to find a computer with access to Wi-Fi.

be synonymous with equality-of-result, overpriced indoctrination echo chambers, where therapy replaced singular rigor and
their tarnished degrees become irrelevant."[1] The author gave no
evidence to justify his dire prediction.

Specific allegations from the Right often rest on shaky foundations. For example, their frequent claims that liberal professors
indoctrinate students ignore a considerable body of evidence that
contradicts such charges. Moreover, the remedies offered by conservative politicians, like those recommended by liberal critics,
are often proposed with little regard for the problems they would
cause and the costs they would entail not only for elites but for
many other colleges as well.

For example, as these lines were being written, Republican
senator Tom Cotton (a graduate of Harvard College and Harvard
Law School) wrote an article announcing his "Student Loan
Reform Act of 2022."[2] His bill would require that all colleges be
guarantors of up to 50 percent of their student loans and pay the
government 25 percent of the losses from each defaulted loan.
He does not mention the inhibiting effects of this proposal on
the willingness of colleges to admit students from low-income
families who require large loans in order to graduate. Nor does he
recognize the ruinous financial effects of his plan on community
colleges and for-profit universities that enroll most of the low-
income, poorly prepared students who need large loans and have
the highest default rates of any colleges.

Although Senator Cotton's proposal was presented as a
"Student Loan Reform Act," his plan is also aimed at putting
a stop to constantly rising college tuitions. The senator claims
that a leading cause of tuition growth is a tendency he describes
as "administrative bloat." To eliminate this problem, he would
require all colleges charging an annual tuition of more than
$20,000 to "gradually eliminate 50 percent of their administrative

staff" within five years or lose their eligibility for government-backed student loans. In addition, he would enact a "luxury tax" of 20 percent on all college tuitions in excess of $40,000 per year and an additional tax of 1 percent on the richest private college endowment incomes. The senator's explanation for imposing these penalties was his claim that "[elite] colleges use their massive fortunes not to serve their students but instead to pay for bloated bureaucracies."[3]

The senator was apparently unaware that elite colleges typically spend much more per student than other colleges on the education of their undergraduates, amounts far greater than the tuitions they charge.[4] Moreover, the only proof he offered for his claim of rampant "administrative bloat" was the fact that the number of staff members in most universities, including elites, has long tended to rise more rapidly than the growth in the numbers of faculty or students. He took no account of the many legitimate reasons why colleges have had to increase their staff more rapidly than their student bodies or their faculties (including the steady growth of government regulations that require additional staff to administer and to submit detailed compliance reports to Washington).* While he may be correct in maintaining that elites have larger staffs than they need, he provided no basis for his startling assumption that 50 percent of their administrators are unnecessary. Nor did he seem to be aware that many of these universities have hired teams from leading consulting firms that

---

*Among the many other reasons for the growth of administrative staff are the cost of maintaining and operating computers and other advanced technology, the cost of treating the large increases in mental health problems of students, the additions to fund-raising staffs that have more than paid for themselves by greatly increasing donations to universities, and the creation of many new athletic teams to comply with the federal requirement to offer equal opportunities to women.

have spent many months trying to identify unnecessary expenses without discovering anything close to the massive "administrative bloat" he alleges.

THE PRECARIOUS SITUATION OF
ELITE UNIVERSITIES

Despite the flaws in the criticisms of both liberals and conservatives, the current situation of elite universities is more precarious than their leaders seem to recognize. As I pointed out in chapter 11, over sixty years have passed since Justice Frankfurter identified four basic academic freedoms—whom to admit as students, whom to appoint to the faculty, how instructors should teach their students, and what they should teach them—that must be immune from government intrusion save for "reasons that are grave and exigent." Since then, judges and other public officials have invaded each of these freedoms with increasing frequency. The Supreme Court itself has recently forbidden the use of race in admitting students to colleges and professional schools. The selection of faculty has enjoyed more freedom from government supervision, but some tenure appointments to a state university faculty have been denied by government-appointed trustees, while Florida's Governor DeSantis has announced his intention to give the president and trustees more power to remove tenured faculty members of state universities. Autonomy in deciding what faculties should teach and how they should conduct their classes has also been compromised in various ways. Several state legislatures have forbidden or simply defunded courses that allegedly teach critical race theory, while Governor DeSantis has issued detailed instructions on how professors in Florida can and cannot teach their students about race relations.

Although most of these interventions apply only to public universities, private institutions are not immune from government regulation. As Senator Cotton's proposal makes clear, governments can tax the endowments of private universities or remove their exemption from taxes if they do not comply with legislative dictates. The Supreme Court has long used its power to interpret legislation to regulate the way these universities can use race in admitting students and, most recently, to forbid racial preferences entirely. President Trump issued regulations requiring the federal government to deny funding to university programs, public or private, that were found to be biased against Israel.

Meanwhile, both liberal and conservative critics have proposed the use of taxes to compel public and private universities to implement drastic proposals for reform. Daniel Markovits of Yale has suggested that the federal government revoke *all* the tax exemptions for selective universities that fail to admit at least half of their students from families in the bottom two-thirds of the income scale. As previously mentioned, Senator Cotton's legislative proposal would impose tax penalties on elite universities that do not gradually eliminate 50 percent of their administrative staff. In short, there are ample ways to impose government mandates on private institutions if legislators choose to use them.

In addition to the threat of government regulation, public opinion has been shifting in ways that make elite universities more vulnerable to political intervention. While higher education enjoyed a favorable reputation in America for many decades, trust in universities began to slip early in this century. This trend has accelerated in recent years. The percentage of Americans who believe that colleges and universities have a positive effect "on the way things are going" in this country dropped from 69 percent in 2020 to 58 percent in 2021 and again to 55 percent in 2022.[5] Meanwhile, the gap between the levels of trust in universities from Democrats and Republicans has widened in recent years to such a point that well over half of all Republicans now lack confidence in higher education.

Several factors appear to contribute to the erosion of public trust. The constant rise of tuitions at a faster rate than increases in the cost of living has doubtless been a contributing factor, as has a growing concern that colleges may not be preparing students adequately for employment. The exceptional loss of trust among many Republicans stems in part from the vast predominance of liberals in college faculties and the belief that professors "bring their political views into the classroom."

The divergent trends in public confidence have obvious political implications. Democratic politicians who represent districts and states with relatively liberal constituencies have not been particularly inclined to target universities. The most drastic recent intrusions by government into the academic affairs of universities have almost all been the work of Republican states, Republican administrations, or Republican-appointed judges. Governor DeSantis from Florida, in particular, has found that a vigorous campaign against the "woke" proclivities of schools and universities is an effective way to motivate his base, which includes large numbers of older White constituents and younger White Christians who have not gone to college.

THE RESPONSE FROM THE ELITES

In the face of serious criticisms from both the Right and the Left, elite universities have been strangely silent. Instead of pointing to their accomplishments or exposing the defects in the reforms suggested by their critics, they have tended to say nothing except when directly challenged in the courts. They have simply hunkered down to wait until the storm clouds pass.

The silence of elites is puzzling. Perhaps their leaders feel that the criticisms and suggested reforms are so obviously impractical and uninformed that they do not deserve a reply. Perhaps they fear that responding will only draw attention to the criticisms and make matters worse. Whatever the reason, saying nothing is a dangerous strategy. If the criticisms are repeated again and again with no response from the institutions involved, many people from all points on the political spectrum will assume that the accusations are valid. Others may look on the silence of the universities as further evidence of a magisterial indifference to criticism.

The silence of elite universities calls to mind the well-known fable of the frog that found itself in a pan of water on top of a hot stove. The frog is initially content to be in its element, immersed in cool water. Before long, however, the water grows progressively warmer but so gradually that the frog does not notice. Eventually, alas, the frog realizes its predicament, but it is then too late and the frog dies.

Fortunately, this unhappy fate is unlikely to befall universities, especially elite universities. They are important to too many people in too many ways to be allowed to die. Nevertheless, the failure to respond more vigorously to the many complaints from their critics increases the risk of further interventions that could seriously hamper their ability to carry out their essential functions. The ultimate danger is that elites will be taxed more and more—by liberals from a desire for greater equality between the various layers of the higher education system and by conservatives, angry that elite universities are so liberal.

This is hardly a propitious time for additional regulations and attendant burdens that will weaken our leading universities unnecessarily.[6] The innovation and expertise that elites supply through their research is particularly important today, when the nation needs to discover how to reform its hugely complicated and expensive health-care system and how best to resist climate change, fix a growing immigration crisis, and alleviate persistent problems of extreme inequality, an inadequate social safety net, child poverty, excessive crime and drug use, and much else. Our most prominent universities, which currently lead the world in the quality of their research, can contribute a lot through additional knowledge and new ideas about the issues facing the nation. Yet their skill in fulfilling this function is not guaranteed, nor is their global reputation assured, especially now that China and Western Europe are rapidly closing the gap with the United States in the quality and quantity of their scientific research while making particular efforts to improve their best universities. As a result, both for their own well-being and for the welfare of society, leading universities need to consider a more substantial effort to protect themselves from the dangers that surround them.

WHAT UNIVERSITIES COULD DO

Building and regaining trust is a difficult task in a time of discontent like the present, when the public is suspicious of most established organizations, and journalists can easily attract approving audiences by describing the follies and misadventures of prominent institutions. No friendly outside entity can be counted on to undertake the hard and patient work required. Leading universities must do the job by themselves. Reminding the public of America's lofty showing in the rankings of the world's best universities will surely not suffice. Elites must engage in serious efforts both to address existing problems in their own behavior and to explore opportunities to serve new needs of genuine value to students and the nation. Fortunately, numerous possibilities exist for pursuing both of these goals.

There are several immediate steps that our leading universities could take to defend themselves better against the risks that confront them. To begin with, they need to recognize that even though most of the attacks on them are exaggerated and though the remedies proposed by critics are often impractical, there is usually a valid problem connected in some way to each of the complaints. Several common practices of admissions offices *are* hard to justify. Although conservative accusations of indoctrination are not convincingly supported by the evidence, it *is* unfortunate that there are so few conservatives within the faculties of elite universities and that many liberal instructors appear to express their political opinions in their classes even when they are not germane to the subject matter of the course. And though the current efforts by elites to promote "diversity, equity, and inclusion" have been launched with the best of intentions, they are too often carried out in ways that compromise the freedom of speech of faculty members and students.

Academic leaders would be well-advised to proceed forthwith to remedy these problems. They should abandon hard-to-defend admissions policies; seek ways to overcome the virtual absence of conservatives in their faculties without compromising their intellectual standards; urge faculty members to refrain from uttering unrelated expressions of political opinion in their classes; and discourage efforts to promote diversity, equity, and inclusion that inhibit freedom of speech. The willingness of elites to acknowledge these problems and make serious efforts to overcome them should help earn them greater trust and respect from the public. Unfortunately, it is already too late to gain much respect from doing away with legacy preferences. Such action will be widely regarded as a response to the mounting pressure to do what should have been done years ago. But it is still possible for elites to remedy other problems and gain recognition for having the resolve to reform themselves without waiting for others to do it for them.

In addition to remedying these mistakes, elite universities could try to demonstrate their commitment to improving the quality of undergraduate education by taking steps, either individually or with others, to strengthen areas of instruction in which they are weak. The most important of these improvements have been discussed in chapter 9—finding better ways to help undergraduates discover a meaningful and satisfying calling after they graduate, providing a basic preparation for all their students to become informed and active citizens in a democratic society, and developing their ability to recognize ethical problems when they arise and to think clearly and carefully about how to respond.

Another intriguing possibility for leading universities to explore arises from the recent discovery by psychologists that various important behaviors and capabilities, such as creativity, empathy, resilience, and conscientiousness, which were long thought to become largely immutable during childhood, continue to be malleable, and hence potentially teachable, at least through early adulthood. Since these capabilities are of great value to students and, in the form of so-called soft skills, to employers as well, concerted effort by leading universities to explore ways to teach them could eventually enhance the benefits of undergraduate education significantly.

Still another important way for leading universities to enhance the quality of education would be to improve the preparation of graduate students and non-tenure-track instructors and provide them with greater opportunities to play a more secure and effective role in teaching undergraduates. If organizations such as the Association of American Universities (AAU) took the lead in mobilizing and encouraging their members to explore these opportunities, they would surely offer a convincing demonstration of how these favored institutions serve the public as well as their students.

In addition to these positive steps to regain the confidence of the public, leaders of elite universities need to be aware of several all-too-common practices that can weaken the reputation of elites and give ammunition to their critics. One such misstep results from a desire to try to satisfy everyone by simultaneously pursuing contradictory policies. For example, as chapter 8 pointed out, some universities have advertised their commitment to unfettered freedom of speech while simultaneously making inroads on the First Amendment in their effort to provide a supportive campus environment for minorities, LGBTQ students, and other identity groups. Another common practice is to announce the impressive intellectual credentials of the entering class while quietly setting aside a substantial number of places each year to legacies, athletes, and children of potential donors. Such inconsistent policies are often confusing and make universities seem devious and hypocritical.

Another practice that can get elite universities in trouble is to settle unpleasant controversies by agreeing to demands from groups of students or faculty without taking adequate account of the risk of creating precedents that may be hard to live with when similar demands are made on future administrations. Awarding reparations without carefully defining the extent of the university's moral responsibility is one example; avoiding trouble by accepting the demands of students to discourage unwelcome speech or rescind invitations to controversial speakers is another; and agreeing to sell the stock of corporations in order to satisfy activist students may eventually prove to be a third.

A very different problem that occurs periodically in research universities is a tendency to respond to complaints about an administrator or a professor who has acted irresponsibly by settling the problem quietly after paying or otherwise silencing the victims in an effort to protect the university's reputation. All too often, of course, the problem eventually comes to light, costing the university large sums of money and, worse yet, undermining trust in the integrity of its leaders. Mishaps of this kind convey a useful message. When scandals occur, the greatest harm to the reputation of the university usually results not from the scandalous behavior itself but from the response of the administration.

If they are not already doing so, presidents of elites should also consider reaching out more often to talk with critics such as politicians, both conservative and liberal, many of whom are graduates of their universities. By doing so, they may better understand the criticisms against them while informing their critics more fully about conditions on their campuses. Reporters and editors from leading newspapers and opinion magazines will often welcome informal conversations with university presidents about controversial problems in higher education. Done properly, such exchanges could eventually help reduce misunderstandings and create greater trust and common ground.

Leading universities also need to make a more determined effort to inform the general public about the good things they are doing. At present, it is hard to find any published account of the many ways by which these universities benefit the public.* Very little has been published about the extraordinary array of extra-curricular programs supported by elites that enable students to help address a variety of human needs and social problems. Little attention has been paid in books and articles to all that many of these universities have done in recent years to increase the number of lower-income students they admit. Someone ought

---

*One obvious exception to this statement is Jonathan Cole's excellent study *The Great American University,* but that book was published fifteen years ago.

to explain why this task is harder than it seems, and how much money and effort elite universities are devoting to increasing opportunity by diversifying their student bodies and making their colleges welcoming and affordable to students from every income level. As I previously mentioned, there are likewise few, if any, published critiques that expose the many flaws of the lotteries and quotas and other schemes that critics suggest for changing the admissions policies of elite universities to educate a more diverse student body. Without such analysis, unsupported criticisms and impractical remedies could eventually gain more credibility than they deserve.

Finally, leading colleges have done too little to make the public aware of the positive efforts that are currently under way to improve teaching and learning. Casual readers and viewers today could easily gain the impression that the most important new developments in undergraduate education are the publication of lists of words that can give offense to others, and the ways by which artificial intelligence is helping students write their term papers without having to use their minds. Media accounts of college life tend to pay much more attention to the occasional student disruption of a controversial speaker or the illegal methods of a dozen celebrity families to get their children admitted to selective universities than they do to describing the remarkable efforts of thousands of student volunteers to help meet the needs of less fortunate members of society.

In fact, many more worthwhile activities are going on in elite universities than most people realize. Building greater confidence by increasing understanding is a delicate task that universities must try to accomplish without sounding defensive, arrogant, or boastful. Success will not come quickly or easily. In the end, however, the saving grace for America's elite universities is that they *are* remarkable institutions and that they *do* contribute to society in many important ways. With enough humility to acknowledge their faults, more determined efforts to improve the quality of education, and greater skill in informing the public of their progress, they should be able to build the trust that will help them survive their current predicament and emerge better and stronger than ever.

NOTES

CHAPTER 1. Why Have Our Leading Universities Been So Successful, and What Responsibilities Do They Owe in Return?

1. See, e.g., Wendy Fischman and Howard Gardner, *The Real World of College: What Higher Education Is and What It Can Be* (2022), pp. 73–114.

2. William C. Kirby, *Empires of Ideas: Creating the Modern University from Germany to America to China* (2022), esp. pp. 267–301.

3. For example, Michael Sandel, *The Tyranny of Merit* (2020); Daniel Markovits, *The Meritocracy Trap: How America's Foundational Myth Feeds Inequality, Dismantles the Middle Class, and Devours the Elite* (2019).

CHAPTER 2. A View from the Bridge

1. I am indebted to James Duderstadt, past president of the University of Michigan, for this chapter title. Duderstadt may in turn have borrowed the words from Arthur Miller's play with the same title.

2. William C. Kirby, *Empires of Ideas: Creating the Modern University from Germany to America to China* (2022), p. 382.

3. A. O. Al-Youbi et al., *The Leading World's Most Innovative Universities* (2021).

4. Jonathan R. Cole, *The Great American University: Its Rise to Prominence, Its Indispensable Role, Why It Must Be Protected* (2009).

5. During the administrations of the last five presidents, 60 graduates of an Ivy League university have been numbered among the 155 appointees to a cabinet position. Audrey W. June and Brian O'Leary, "Where 5 Presidents, Cabinets Went to College," *Chronicle of Higher Education*, January 22, 2021, p. 30.

6. Ernest Pascarella and Patrick Terenzini, *How College Affects Students*, vol. 2, *A Third Decade of Research* (2005), pp. 471–76.

7. Caroline Hoxby, *The Effects of Geographical Integration and Increasing Competition in the Market for College Education* (1998).

8. See, e.g., Brandon Busteed, "Top 25 Universities According to Alumni Ratings," *Forbes*, October 21, 2020.

9. See, e.g., Joshua Kim and Edward Maloney, *Learning Innovation and the Future of Higher Education* (2020).

10. These figures come from Rahem D. Hamid and Nia L. Orakwue, "Harvard College Accepts Record-Low 3.19% of Applicants to Class of 2026," *Harvard Crimson*, April 1, 2022, https://www.thecrimson.com/article/2022/4/1/admissions-class-of-2026/.

CHAPTER 3. Choosing Whom to Admit to Elite Universities in an Age of Extreme Inequality

1. See, e.g., Michael Sandel, *The Tyranny of Merit* (2021); Daniel Markovits, *The Meritocracy Trap: How America's Foundational Myth Feeds Inequality, Dismantles the Middle Class, and Devours the Elite* (2019).

2. Raj Chetty et al., "Mobility Report Card: The Role of College in Intergenerational Mobility" (NBER Working Paper no. 23618, 2018).

3. See, e.g., Lani Guinier and Susan P. Sturm, *Who's Qualified? A New Democracy Forum on the Future of American Democracy* (2001); Lani Guinier, *The Tyranny of the Meritocracy: Democratizing Higher Education in America* (2015).

4. James L. Shulman and William G. Bowen, *The Game of Life: College Sports and Educational Values* (2001), p. 75.

5. Christopher Avery, Andrew Fairbanks, and Richard J. Zeckhauser, *The Early Admissions Game: Joining the Elite* (2009).

6. Julie Park, *Race on Campus: Debunking Myths with Data* (2018).

7. Caroline Hoxby and Christopher Avery, "The Missing One-Offs: The Hidden Supply of High-Achieving, Low-Income Students" (Brookings Papers on Economic Activity, Spring 2013).

8. Caroline Hoxby and Sarah Turner, "Informing Students about Their College Options: A Proposal for Broadening the Expanding College Opportunities Project" (Hamilton Project, June 2013).

9. Matt Barnum, "The College Board Tried a Simple, Cheap, Research-Backed Way to Push Low-Income Kids into Better Colleges. It Didn't Work," *Chalkbeat*, May 31, 2019, https://www.chalkbeat.org/2019/5/31/21121043/the-college-board-tried-a-simple-cheap-research-backed-way-to-push-low-income-kids-into-better-colle.

10. Posse Foundation, www.possefoundation.org; GuideStar, www
.guidestar.org.

11. Selective universities could try to protect themselves and limit the number of low-income students by awarding them so little financial aid that they could not afford to enroll. Government officials would presumably bring suit to prevent universities from circumventing the purpose of the lottery system in this obvious way. The ultimate result would be to draw the government even further into the regulation of university operations as public officials began to review financial aid procedures in order to eliminate any bias against the neediest applicants.

12. Sandel, *The Tyranny of Merit.*

13. David Kirp, "Why Stanford Should Clone Itself," *New York Times,* April 6, 2021.

14. Markovits, *The Meritocracy Trap.*

15. In recommending that elites fill their quota of lower-income students by enlarging the size of their student bodies (presumably in professional schools as well as colleges), Markovits fails to ask whether the nation truly needs additional graduates in several of the occupations involved. Should universities produce many more PhDs when current graduates cannot find tenure-track positions and must settle for insecure and poorly paid jobs as adjunct instructors? Should elite law schools admit more students when many law graduates today cannot find jobs with salaries sufficient to allow them to repay their educational loans? Should elite business schools produce more MBAs when many employers are already questioning the value of a business school degree and advising college graduates to remain at work and learn what they need on the job?

16. It is even uncertain what effect Markovits's proposal would have on colleges that are not extremely selective. If elite colleges expand their size to meet his quota, less selective colleges could find themselves compelled to admit weaker students with greater financial needs, since the most selective universities would presumably try to meet the prescribed quota by recruiting as many students as possible from just below the top one-third of the income scale in order to limit the cost of compliance. As a result, the Markovits proposal could have the perverse effect of bankrupting many colleges that are less selective and less wealthy, since most of these colleges do not have huge endowments and are already having to give large discounts in the form of scholarships to applicants with above-average incomes to attract enough students and receive enough tuition money to survive. Even some highly selective public institutions, such as the flagship state universities, might have to make painful budget cuts unless their governments provided them with larger appropriations to meet their increased costs.

17. Raj Chetty, David J. Deming, and John W. Deming, "Diversifying Society's Leaders? The Causal Effects of Admission to Highly Selective Private Colleges," National Bureau of Economic Research, Working Paper 31492 (July 2023).

18. Sandy Baum and Michael McPherson, *Can College Level the Playing Field? Higher Education in an Unequal Society* (2022), p. 14.

CHAPTER 4. Student Protests and the Role of Elite Universities in Combating Evil and Injustice in the World

1. W. Bentley McLeod and Miguel Urquiola, "Why Does the United States Have the Best Research Universities? Incentives, Resources and Virtuous Circles," *Journal of Economic Perspectives* 35 (Winter 2005): 185, 187–88; Philippe Aghion et al., "The Governance and Performance of Universities: Evidence from Europe and the U.S.," *Economic Policy* 25 (January 2010): 7–59.

2. Matthew A. Winkler, "Texans Pay for a 'War on Woke,'" *The Week*, February 24, 2023, p. 34.

CHAPTER 5. Reparations

1. See, e.g., Alfred L. Brophy, *Reparations: Pro and Con* (2006); Craig S. Wilder, *Ebony and Ivy: Race, Slavery, and the Troubled History of American Universities* (2013).

2. "Report of the Presidential Committee on Harvard & the Legacy of Slavery" (2022).

3. Ibid., chap. 7, "Recommendations to the President and Fellows of Harvard University."

4. *Regents of the University of California v. Bakke*, 438 U.S. 265 (1978).

INTRODUCTION TO PART III

1. Maureen Dowd, "The Marjorie Taylor Greene-ing of America," *New York Times*, November 5, 2022.

2. Michael Stratford, "Trump Vows to Go after 'Radical Left' Colleges, Echoing DeSantis Approach," *Politico*, May 2, 2023, https://www.politico.com/news/2023/05/02/trump-colleges-desantis-00095007.

3. Kim Parker, Pew Research Center, "The Growing Partisan Divide: Views of Higher Education" (August 19, 2019), https://www.pewresearch.org/social-trends/2019/08/19/the-growing-partisan-divide-in-views-of-higher-education-2/.

4. Ibid.

5. Asma Khalid, "How White Liberals Became Woke," *NPR Politics Newsletter*, October 1, 2019, https://www.npr.org/2019/10/01/763383478/how-white-liberals -became-woke-radically-changing-their-outlook-on-race.

6. Ibid.

CHAPTER 6. Are College Students Being Indoctrinated by Liberal Professors?

1. Neil Gross and Solon Simmons, "The Social and Political Views of American Professors" (National Bureau of Economic Research Working Paper 15954, 2007), p. 70.

2. Ellen Bara Stolzenberg et al., *Undergraduate Teaching Faculty: The Higher Education Research Institute Faculty Survey, 2016–17* (2019), p. 17.

3. *New York Times*, citing German Lopez, "The Morning Newsletter, Fox News for Universities," February 17, 2023.

4. Meimei Xu, "More Than 80 Percent of Surveyed Harvard Faculty Identify as Liberal," *Harvard Crimson*, July 13, 2022.

5. Stanley Rothman and S. Robert Lichtman, "The Vanishing Conservative—Is There a Glass Ceiling?" in *The Politically Correct University: Problems, Scope, and Reforms*, ed. Robert Maranto, Richard E. Redding, and Federic M. Hess (2009), p. 60.

6. Alyssa N. Rockenbach, Matthew J. Mayhew, Kevin Singer, and Laura S. Dahl, "Professors Change Few Minds on Politics—but Conservative Ones May Have More Influence," *Washington Post*, March 2, 2020.

7. Matthew J. Mayhew et al., "Does College Turn People into Liberals?" *The Conversation*, February 2, 2018.

8. Matthew Mayhew and Alyssa Rockenbach, "Does 4 Years of College Make Students More Liberal?" *The Conversation*, September 8, 2020.

9. Rockenbach et al., "Professors Change Few Minds." In fact, only 10 percent of students felt any pressure to change their opinions to align more closely with the views of their professor. Of these students, a slightly higher percentage were liberal rather than conservative.

10. "Half of College Students Surveyed Fear Expressing Their Ideas in Classrooms," Intelligent.com, September 1, 2021, https://www.intelligent.com/ college-students-fear-expressing-ideas-in-classroom/.

11. Ibid.

12. See, e.g., Conor Friedersdorf, "Evidence That Conservative Students Do Self-Censor," *Atlantic*, February 16, 2020.

13. Knight Foundation survey, 2019, cited by Samuel Abrams and Amna Khalid, "Are Colleges and Universities Too Liberal? What the Research Says about the Political Composition of Campuses and Campus Climate," American Enterprise Institute, October 21, 2020.

14. Mayhew and Rockenbach, "Does 4 Years of College Make Students More Liberal?"

15. Matthew Woessner and April Kelly-Woessner, "Left Pipeline: Why Conservatives Don't Get Doctorates," in Maranto et al., *The Politically Correct University*, p. 38.

16. Gross and Simmons, "The Social and Political Views of American Professors," pp. 67–70.

CHAPTER 7. The Campaign against Racial Preferences as Elite Universities Seek to Diversify Their Student Bodies

1. Regents of the University of California v. Bakke, 438 U.S. 265 (1978).

2. William G. Bowen and Derek Bok, *The Shape of the River: Long-Term Consequences of Considering Race in College and University Admissions,* Twentieth Anniversary Edition (2019).

3. Ibid., pp. 54–68.

4. Ibid., pp. 194–205.

5. Ibid., pp. 241–48.

6. Ibid., pp. 72–86.

7. Ibid., pp. 72–78.

8. Claude M. Steele and Joshua Aronson, "Stereotype Threat and the Intellectual Test Performance of African Americans," *Journal of Personality and Social Psychology* 69 (1995): 797.

9. Grutter v. Bollinger, 539 U.S. 306 (2003).

10. Matthew J. Mayhew et al., *How College Affects Students,* vol. 3 (2016), p. 550.

11. Ibid., p. 552.

12. Melvin Urofsky, *The Affirmative Action Puzzle: A Living History from Reconstruction to Today* (2020), p. 465.

13. Bowen and Bok, *The Shape of the River,* p. 145

CHAPTER 8. Have Elite Universities Sacrificed Freedom of Speech in Their Effort to Provide a Supportive Environment for All Students?

1. Claude M. Steele and Joshua Aronson, "Stereotype Threat and the Intellectual Test Performance of African Americans," *Journal of Personality and Social Psychology* 69 (1995): 797.

2. See, e.g., Toni Schmader and William L. Hall, "Stereotype Threat in School and at Work: Putting Science into Practice," *Policy Insights from the Behavioral and Brain Sciences* 1 (2014): 30.

3. Alan Charles Kors and Harvey A. Silverglate, *The Shadow University: The Betrayal of Liberty on America's Campuses* (1998).

4. See, e.g., Richard H. Fallon Jr., "Sexual Harassment, Content Neutrality, and the First Amendment Dog That Didn't Bark," *Supreme Court Review* (1994): 1.

5. Davis v. Monroe County Board of Education, 526 U.S. 629, 651 (1991).

6. Garcetti v. Ceballos, 547 U.S. 410 (2006).

7. Robert Soave, "MIT Canceled a Professor's Guest Lecture Because He Opposes Race-Based Admissions," *Reason* (October 21, 2021).

8. John Villasenor, "Views among College Students Regarding the First Amendment: Results from a New Survey," Brookings Institution, September 18, 2017.

9. Derek Bok, *Higher Education in America* (2013), p. 359.

10. Ibid.

11. Neil Gross and Solon Simmons, "The Social and Political Views of American Professors" (National Bureau of Economic Research Working Paper 15954, 2007), p. 70.

12. Quoted in Alexander Kafka, "Academic Freedom Is on the Ropes," *Chronicle of Higher Education*, May 27, 2021.

13. John McWhorter, "Academics Are Really, Really Worried about Their Freedom," *Atlantic*, September 1, 2020.

14. Geoffrey R. Stone, "Free Speech on Campus: A Report from the University Faculty Committee" (University of Chicago School of Law, 2015).

15. It is interesting to note that despite the stout defense of free speech by the University of Chicago, graduation rates of Black students are almost 90 percent, only several percentage points below the rate for Whites. Moreover, it is likewise true that at many other elite universities, the graduation rates for Whites and Blacks are virtually identical. According to a recent report by the Lumina Foundation and the Gallup organization, Black students are much less likely than Whites to complete their studies and obtain a degree at community colleges and for-profit universities either because they feel discriminated against or because they have jobs or other obligations in addition to their college classes. Jalen Brown, "Black Students Are Less Likely to Attain College Degrees Because of Discrimination and External Responsibilities, Study Finds," CNN, February 9, 2023.

16. See, e.g., Higher Education Research Institute (UCLA), "Findings from the 2015 College Senior Survey" (2015).

17. See, e.g., Conor Friedersdorf, "Evidence That Conservative Students Really Do Self-Censor," *Atlantic*, February 16, 2020; Liam Quinn, "Less Than

Half of Republican College Students Feel Safe Sharing Their Beliefs on Campus, New Survey Finds," *Fox News*, March 12, 2019.

18. See Elizabeth Redden, "Georgetown Professor Fired for Statement about Black Students," *Inside Higher Education*, March 11, 2021.

19. "Excerpts from the 1940 *Statement of Principles on Academic Freedom and Tenure*," in Matthew W. Finkin and Robert C. Post, *For the Common Good: Principles of American Academic Freedom* (2009), pp. 184–85.

20. James Freeman, "Most U.S. College Students Afraid to Disagree with Professors," *Wall Street Journal*, October 26, 2018.

21. Quoted in Stone, "Free Speech on Campus."

CHAPTER 9. Should Our Leading Universities Do More to Improve the Quality of Education?

1. Philip S. Babcock and Mindy Marks, "The Falling Time Cost of College: Evidence from Half a Century of Time Use Data," *Review of Economics and Statistics* 93 (2011): 468.

2. See, e.g., Ernest T. Pascarella and Patrick T. Terenzini, *How College Affects Students*, vol. 2, *A Third Decade of Research* (2005), p. 158.

3. Jack H. Schuster and Martin J. Finkelstein, *The American Faculty: Restructuring of Academic Work and Careers* (2006), p. 69.

4. "A Turning Point in Higher Education: The Inaugural Address of Charles William Eliot as President of Harvard College," October 19, 1869 (1969), p. 11.

5. Ellen Bara Stolzenberg et al., *Undergraduate Teaching Faculty: The Higher Education Research Institute Faculty Survey, 2016–17* (2019).

6. Schuster and Finkelstein, *The American Faculty*.

7. Stolzenberg et al., *Undergraduate Teaching Faculty*.

8. Pascarella and Terenzini, *How College Affects Students*, vol. 2.

9. The evidence is summarized in Derek Bok, *Higher Expectations: Can Colleges Teach Students What They Need to Know in the Twenty-First Century?* (2020), pp. 95–122.

10. William James, "The Ph.D. Octopus" (1903).

11. See, e.g., Paul D. Umbach, "How Effective Are They? Exploring the Impact of Contingent Faculty on Undergraduate Education," *Review of Higher Education* (Winter 2007): 9.

12. Ibid.

13. Adrianna Kezar, Daniel Maxey, and Elizabeth Holcomb, *The Professoriate Reconsidered: A Study of New Faculty Models* (2015).

CHAPTER 10. The Many Sins of Intercollegiate Athletics

1. James L. Shulman and William G. Bowen, *The Game of Life: College Sports and Educational Values* (2001), p. 319.

2. William G. Bowen and Sarah A. Levin, *Reclaiming the Game: College Sport and Educational Values* (2003).

3. Ibid., p. 328.

4. Ibid.

5. Ibid.

6. William G. Bowen and Derek Bok, *The Shape of the River: Long-Term Effects of Considering Race in College and University Admissions* (1998), pp. 242, 246.

7. Shulman and Bowen, *The Game of Life*, pp. 182, 265.

CHAPTER 11. Dire Thoughts before Daybreak about the Future of Elite Universities

1. Like students, presidents display far more confidence in the abilities of their recent graduates than executives of the companies that employ them.

How Well Prepared Are Recent Graduates?

	Presidents	Employers
Very well prepared	23%	2%
Well prepared	50%	18%
Prepared	25%	49%
Unprepared	2%	28%
Very unprepared	0%	3%

2. *Sweezy v. New Hampshire*, 354 U.S. 234 (1957).

CONCLUSION. What Elite Universities Could Do

1. Victor D. Hanson, "The Woke University Implosion—and What Comes Next," *New York Post*, December 25, 2022.

2. Tom Cotton, "The End of Academia's Golden Age," *Fox News*, September 21, 2022. For another example, see Ayelet Sheffey, "Josh Hawley Introduces a Bill to Hold Colleges Accountable for Surging Student Debt Instead of 'Teaching Nonsense Like Men Can Get Pregnant,'" *Business Insider*, September 21, 2022.

3. Cotton, "The End of Academia's Golden Age."

4. Caroline M. Hoxby, "The Changing Selectivity of American Colleges," *Journal of Economic Perspectives* 23 (Fall 2009): 109.

5. Karin Fischer, "America's Confidence in Higher Education Drops Sharply," *Chronicle of Higher Education,* July 26, 2022.

6. The most careful recent studies to determine why the leading American universities dominate the global rankings for the quality of their research and education attribute this success to the greater autonomy of private research universities in the United States. Miguel Urquiola, *Markets, Minds, and Money: Why America Leads the World in University Research* (2020), and Philippe Aghion et al., "The Governance and Performance of Universities: Evidence from Europe and the U.S.," *Economic Policy* 25 (January 2010): 7–59.

ACKNOWLEDGMENTS

———

This book could not have been written, let alone published, without the help of many friends and supporters. First of all, I must warmly thank Peter Dougherty, recently retired from the Princeton University Press, who was my editor for twenty-five years. Peter helped me reconceive the focus and content of my manuscript after I had made an awkward effort to combine a memoir with a series of essays drawn from my twenty-five years of academic administration. No longer at Princeton, he kindly volunteered to help me place the revised manuscript in the capable hands of Yale University Press.

I must also give thanks to my friends and longtime Harvard colleagues Bill Fitzsimmons and Charles Fried, who read and commented on individual chapters of the book. My former student and the founder and president of the Posse Foundation, Debbie Bial, read my chapter on college admissions and advised me on the challenge of recruiting and preparing inner-city students who can flourish at highly selective colleges. I owe a special debt to my wife and three children, each of whom read various chapters of the book and gave me much useful advice about how to improve what I had written.

In addition, I must convey my gratitude and appreciation to Connie Higgins for her invaluable assistance at every stage of preparing this manuscript. Connie and I have worked together for the past thirty years. Without her help in transforming my all-but-illegible drafts into polished and readable pages, I doubt that I could have published any of the ten or more books I have written over the past three decades.

I am also grateful to Seth Ditchik, Josh Panos, Ann Twombly, Joyce Ippolito, and their colleagues at the Yale University Press who have transformed my manuscript into a finished volume. They have been consistently helpful at every stage, from finding anonymous readers to comment on my manuscript to adjusting the production schedule to accommodate my desire to delay publication until after the Supreme Court announced its decision on the legality of admissions preferences for minority applicants in *Students for Fair Admissions v. President and Fellows of Harvard College*.

Finally, I must offer thanks to the members of Harvard's governing boards for granting me the privilege of spending my entire working life in the oldest of the remarkable institutions that are the subject of this book.

INDEX

A

AAU (Association of American Universities), 201

AAUP (Association of American University Professors), 113, 125

academic freedom: AAUP definition of, 125; autonomy of professors and university over course offerings and content, 62, 113; decline in confidence in, 116–17, 125; Frankfurter's recognition of, 184–85, 195; practices at odds with, 77, 114–16, 202; threats to, 116–17. *See also* free speech

academic performance. *See* grades; graduation rates

ACT tests. *See* SAT/ACT tests

adjunct lecturers. *See* non-tenure-track instructors

admissions: athletics and, 30, 32–33, 154–55, 161, 164–65, 172; auctions of entry spots, 32; challenges after *Students for Fair Admissions* case (2023), 104–8; current predicament, 36–38; early admission practice, 33–34; essays by applicants, 29, 208n17; faculty children, preferential treatment of, 34; false claims of applicants, 210n17; government intervention in, 37; liberal critique, 25, 27–54, 192; lottery system, 43–48, 192, 204, 209n11; low-income applicants and, 13, 20–21, 24, 28–30, 36–38, 50, 193, 203; meritocracy, attempts to abolish, 47–48, 49, 104; number of applicants to, 18, 36, 140; questions on student involvement in furthering equality and inclusion, 115; recommendations for, 38–42, 52–54, 200; selection criteria, 7–8; special nature and needs of college as factor, 44; Supreme Court decisions against racial preference in, 104–5, 195–96; wealthy students'

155; recruiting of players, 154, 158, 162, 163–64; reforms, feasibility and likelihood of, 164–65, 171–72; salaries for athletes while in college, 159; SAT/ACT test scores of athletes, 32, 154–57, 161–62, 165, 167; satisfaction from participation and team bonds, 170; scholarships for, 154; school spirit and, 169; special course offerings for athletes, 154; uniform academic requirements and, 154–56; unionization of college players, 159–60, 175; women athletes, 163, 165, 194

attorneys, Blacks as, 94, 96

auctions of entry spots, 32

Avery, Christopher, 39

B

Bakke case. *See Regents of the University of California v. Bakke*

Baum, Sandy, 53

Bierce, Ambrose, 75

Blacks: graduation rates from elite colleges and, 100, 211n15; at Harvard Law School, 94–98; Harvard recruitment of students, 78; Harvard reparations fund, 72; recruitment of faculty and staff, 77; standardized testing and, 35; "stereotype threats" and, 100–101, 110. *See also* racial discrimination; racial diversity in admissions

Blum, Edward, 104–5

Bok, Derek: *Higher Expectations: Can Colleges Teach Students What*

They Need to Know in the Twenty-First Century?, 15; *The Shape of the River* (with Bowen), 35, 99–102, 107

Bowen, William G. (Bill), 35, 99–102, 107, 160–67

boycotts of companies engaged in questionable activities, 55–56

branch or satellite campuses, 47–48, 192

British universities, 5

Brookings Institution survey of undergraduates on free speech (2017), 116

Brooks, Arthur C., 92

Brown University: lowering number of teams, 168; student athletes suing for antitrust violations, 166

Bryn Mawr College, 99

Burns, Nick, 191–92

Bush, George H. W., 110

Bush, George W., 88

business schools: ethics courses, 134; social responsibility courses, 134; teaching approach in, 140

Byers, Walter, 162

C

Calarco, Jessica, 192

California Institute of Technology (Caltech), 22

California's prohibition on racial preferences for admission to public universities, 106

Cambridge University, 5

"cancel culture." *See* political correctness

discipline: of faculty expressing insensitive or disrespectful views, 124–25, 127; of students expressing hostile or disrespectful views, 124

discrimination. *See* racial discrimination; racial diversity in admissions; *specific ethnic/racial groups*

diversity: education to learn benefits of, 24, 78, 101–2; free speech policy and, 121, 200; Harvard Law School and, 94–98; hostile or disrespectful behavior toward minority students, 109–11, 116, 123–25. *See also* gender and sexual orientation; racial discrimination; racial diversity in admissions; women; *specific category or ethnic/racial group*

diversity, equity, and inclusion policy: defunding state universities with, 185; freedom of speech reconciled with, 115, 120, 129, 185, 200, 202

divestment of university holdings, 55–65; academic freedom and, 61–62; current reflections on, 65–68; decision-making process, recommendations for, 67–68; environmentally responsible investing, 65, 192; financial consequences of, 60–61; questionable effectiveness of, 59–64, 66; retribution against university for, 62–63, 66, 68; social responsibility and, 57, 59, 63, 65, 67; student protests seeking, 55–65; in tobacco companies, 57; trustees' role, 68

donors: admission preferences for children of, 31–32, 52, 181; fund-raising, 6, 181–84; immoral means to accrue wealth, 74–76; as trustees, 182; university condemnation for conduct of, 78, 80. *See also* endowments

dropout rates, 1, 110, 133, 147

Duke University, 155

Dunlop, John, 175

E

early admissions, 33–34

Edwards, Mickey, 91

Eliot, Charles W., 67, 139

elite universities: accomplishments of, 17–24, 52, 198, 203; administrative staff, 121, 179–80, 194, 196; burden of success, 16; criticisms of, viii, 2, 16, 196; economic benefits generated by, 11–12; educational reforms post–Civil War, 133, 135; exaggerated and misleading commentary about, 191; government intervention, possibility of, 198; graduation rates of Black students, 100, 211n15; justification for, 7–10; lack of response to criticisms, 197–99; loss of trust in, 196–97; need to address loss of public trust, 199–205; obligations incurred by, 2–3, 10–16; problems facing without evident solutions, 173–89; reputation of, 196, 202–4; shared characteristics of, 1–2; success of, 5–16, 204; use of term "elite," 1. *See also* quality of undergraduate education

ance with, 113, 119–22, 126, 130;
alternative classes created in
reaction to, 113, 115, 127; cancel-
lation of speakers for controversial views or past statements/
conduct, 114; civil libertarians
on, 110–11; clarity of university
goals in policy on, 120, 127–28;
in conflict with minority rights,
109–10, 115, 120, 122, 125, 129,
185, 200, 202; confusion of
present approaches, 113–17, 129,
202; constitutional guarantee
of, 111–13, 115–16, 121–23, 125,
127, 129; discipline of faculty
for insensitive or disrespectful
speech, 124–25, 127; discipline
of students for hostile or disrespectful speech, 124; diversity,
equity, and inclusion policy and,
115, 120, 129, 185, 200; faculty
speech and, 124–29; harassment
vs., 111, 123, 130; movie *Othello*
with actor in blackface prohibited, 114–15, 124; peer response
to flagrant examples of prejudice, 122; practices at odds with,
77, 114–16, 202; recommendations for university policy, 119–
29; self-censoring and fears of
expressing unpopular opinions,
117, 123, 128; sexual harassment
and, 111; student speech policy
and speech codes, 87–89, 110–11,
117, 121–24; Supreme Court on,
111–13; University of Chicago
report on (2015), 117–19; untenured faculty and, 61–62, 66, 68;
workshops on issues of race and

gender, 121. *See also* academic
freedom
Friday, William C. (Bill), 153–54
funding and fund-raising challenges, 6, 132, 179–84. *See also*
endowments

G

Garcetti v. Ceballos (2006), 112
Gates, Henry Louis, Jr., 96
gender and sexual orientation, 84,
112; hostile or disrespectful behavior toward, 109–11; restricted
discussion of, 117, 202
Georgia State University, 133
Gergen, David, 92
Germany: as model for America's
universities, 135; seeking to develop elite universities, 10
Goldman Sachs, 62
government intervention: defunding
state universities with diversity,
equity, and inclusion programs,
185; faculty appointments and,
90–91; Frankfurter on limited
role in university affairs, 184–85;
legacy admissions and, 38; opposed to race in curriculum or
critical race theory, 91, 185, 187,
195; political shifts, effect on
higher education, 187; race as
factor in admissions, state laws
banning, 106–8; by Republican
states, administrations, or judges,
197; threat of, 185–87, 195–96, 98;
university investment decisions
and, 62–63, 66; vulnerability to,
37, 68, 132

public universities (*continued*)
ships and, 154; curriculum and teaching loads regulated by state laws, 185; endowments of, 6; expanding size of study body to increase number of low-income students, 209n16; free speech rights in, 111–12; fund-raising amounts, 180; government intervention in curriculum of, 90, 112

Purdue University, 117

Q

quality of undergraduate education, 131, 133–52; American system, post–Civil War development of, 133, 135; artificial intelligence and, 149, 204; career choice and, 134; centers for innovation in teaching, 144–46; challenges and problems in need of solutions, 151–52; civic education and, 15, 134, 137, 141–42, 149; continuous quality improvement efforts, 143–44, 149–50; critical thinking, development of, 134, 142, 144, 149; curriculum at elite universities, 135–43; ethical judgment, development of, 131, 134, 142; faculty resistance to change and, 136–41, 146; governance of undergraduate education and, 150–51; innovations at elite schools, lack of, 133, 139, 143; lecturing as teaching method, 136, 139–40; non-tenure-track instructors and, 146–50; psychological development during college years and, 142–43, 201; reforms needed to improve, 143–51, 201; replacing part-time with full-time teaching faculty, 149; research to obtain data to address, 143–44, 169; studying habits and, 9, 19, 134; training PhD students to teach, 145. *See also* faculty; non-tenure-track instructors

R

race in curriculum: critical race theory and, 91, 185, 187, 195; free speech policy and, 121; minefield created when discussing, 117; state defunding programs, 185, 195; state power to dictate what is taught, 112; teaching of history of racial discrimination, 90, 96

racial discrimination, 69–70; course readings with "sensitive" words, 128; Harvard report on (2022), 72–81; in hiring of faculty, 91; speech or conduct constituting, 109–10, 113–14, 124–27; standardized testing and, 35; teaching of history of, 90, 96. *See also* critical race theory; diversity, equity, and inclusion policy; racial diversity in admissions; "stereotype threats"; *specific ethnic/racial groups*

racial diversity in admissions, 94–108; athletics and, 33; Bok and Bowen's book *The Shape of the River* on, 99–103; conservative opponents to race-sensitive admissions, 98; continuation of battle over, 104–8; demands of students for Black faculty and curriculum changes, 96; demise of preferential admissions, 104–8; democracy's need for, 101–2; efforts to promote, 20–21, 37–38, 73, 104; elite universities' commitment to, 108; fight for racial preference, 97–103; Harvard University's policy, 22, 73, 94, 98; justification for, 13–14, 103, 107; as moral responsibility of universities, 13–14; race's impact on applicant as factor in admissions selection, 104–8; *Students for Fair Admissions v. Harvard* (2023), 104–8, 195–96; Supreme Court decisions restricting race as factor, 104–8, 195–96; University of Michigan case (*Grutter v. Bollinger* [2003]), 101. *See also* affirmative action

Reagan, Ronald, 88

Regents of the University of California v. Bakke (1978), 80, 97–98, 104

reparations, 26, 69–81; affirmative action as, 77–79; campaign to obtain from elite universities, 71–72; climate change and, 80–81; Harvard 2022 report and, 72–81; history of, 70–71; lack of standing or lapsed statutes of limitations, 70–71; university's moral responsibility and, 73–77, 202; White responsibility and, 79–80. *See also* Alaska Native Claims Settlement Act

Republicans: intervention in university governance, 90; opinions on higher education, 83, 196–97. *See also* conservative beliefs; conservative critique

research: America's preeminence in, 17–18, 52, 199; benefits to society, 12–13; businesses situating near research universities, 11; faculty balancing teaching and, 19–20, 135–36; grants for, 182; informing public policy through, 58, 66; international students and collaboration with U.S. colleagues, 9; reputation of elite universities for, 7, 11, 136, 140

Rhodes Scholarships, 18

Rockefeller, John D., 75

Roksa, Josipa, 19

Rondeau, Kris, 176

Royall, Isaac, 75

S

Sandel, Michael, 46–47, 49

SAT/ACT tests: in admissions decision making, 29, 34–35, 38, 43–44, 106; athletes and, 32, 154–57, 161–62, 165, 167; criticism of, 29, 34–35; predictive value of, 34, 36, 43, 100, 106, 110, 163; prep course boost and, 35, 106

scandals, response of university to, 183, 203

Schumer, Chuck, 22

segregation patterns, 102, 107

settlement of claims to silence victims, 183, 202–3

sexual abuse or assaults on campus, 169, 177, 183

sexual harassment, 111, 177

Shockley, William B., 77, 127

Silicon Valley, 11

Silverglate, Harvey, 110

Simpson, Alan, 91

slavery, 26, 69–81; Harvard report (2022) on moral responsibility, 72–81. *See also* reparations
social justice, 25, 72
social media attacks, 123
social responsibility, 12–15, 134. *See also* divestment of university holdings; reparations
Sotomayor, Sonia, 22
South Africa: apartheid policy, end of, 64; Harvard scholarships for students from, 65; protests against companies doing business in, 56–58, 64
Southern New Hampshire University, 133
standardized entrance exams, 44
standardized tests. *See* SAT/ACT tests
Stanford, Leland, 75
Stanford University: admissions rate, 18; athlete admissions, 155; attempt to lower number of athletic teams, 168; environmentally responsible investing, 65; free speech policy, 127; Shockley on faculty, 77, 127
Steele, Claude, 100–101, 110
Steiner, Daniel, 98
"stereotype threats," 100–101, 110
stolen art, 76
strikes, 173–74, 178–79. *See also* unionization
student loan reform, 193–94
Student Loan Reform Act of 2022 (proposed), 193–94
student protests and demands, 26, 55–68; causes students protesting, 56, 59–60; contrasting views about, 56–65, 177–78; disadvantages of acceding to, 66–67, 202;

over tuition costs during pandemic, 174–75, 178–79. *See also* divestment of university holdings
students: conservative students, 87–89; disproportionate share of most academically talented in elite institutions, 8–9; filming liberal indoctrination by faculty, 90; foreign students, 9–10, 146; likelihood of later success of, 8–9, 13, 19; older students seeking to acquire new skills, 149; peer response to flagrant examples of prejudice, 122; speech policy and free speech, 87–89, 117, 121–24; study habits of, 9, 19, 134; volunteer activities by, 23–24. *See also* admissions; graduate (PhD) students; student protests and demands
Students for Fair Admissions v. Harvard (2023), 104–8, 195–96
Supreme Court: on affirmative action based on race, 104–8, 195–96; on college athlete endorsement and image ownership rights, 159; on free speech in university environment, 111–13; harassment defined by, 111, 123; justices graduating from Yale or Harvard Law School, 22, 109
Suzman, Helen, 64
Sweezy v. New Hampshire (1957), 184–85

T

tax exemptions, 11–12, 196
teaching: centers for innovation in, 144–46; of creativity and

Urofsky, Melvin, 103
U.S. News & World Report rankings, 35

V

Vance, J. D., 83
Vietnam War, 55

W

Washington University in St. Louis, 171
wealth: advantages in admissions process, 29–30, 31–32, 34–35, 52–53, 181; immoral means to accrue, 74–76; perpetuation of, 25–26; racial disparities in, 108
welfare programs, disproportionate benefit to Black Americans, 71
Wesleyan University, 99
"woke." *See* political correctness

women: in college athletics, 163, 165, 194; hiring of women in faculty and administration, 121; hostile or disrespectful behavior toward, 109–11, 116; in math, 100–101; sexual assaults/abuse on campus, 169, 177; sexual harassment of female students, 111. *See also* gender and sexual orientation
women's studies programs, 136

Y

Yale University, 22, 28, 65, 99, 178

Z

Zimbalist, Andrew, 158